Play It as It Lies

Play It as It Lies

GOLF AND THE SPIRITUAL LIFE

Mike Linder

Westminster John Knox Press
Louisville, Kentucky

First published in 1996 by miclin publishing.

Book design by Sharon Adams
Cover design by Jennifer K. Cox
Cover art courtesy of Picture Network International Ltd.
Backcover art © 1999 PhotoDisc, Inc.

Published by Westminster John Knox Press
Louisville, Kentucky

This book is printed on acid-free paper that meets the American
Natational Standards Institute Z39.48 standard. ∞

PRINTED IN THE UNITED STATES OF AMERICA
99 00 01 02 03 04 05 06 07 08 — 10 9 8 7 6 5 4 3 2 1

Library of Congress Cataloging-in-Publication Data

Linder, Mike.
 Play it as it lies : golf and the spiritual life / Mike Linder. —
1st ed.
  p. cm.
 ISBN 0-664-25822-0 (alk. paper)
  1. Golf—Psychological aspects. 2. Golfers—Conduct
of life.
 I. Title.
GV979.P75L55 1999
796.352'01'9—dc21   98-50849

for
Ernie Newton
and
John Canary
whose lessons
about golf
and mystery
continue to sink in

CONTENTS

TEE TIME

I should begin by admitting that I am more than a little biased. Though I have played many other games and even been a bit fanatical about some of them, golf holds a special place in my heart. I love to play the game, to watch it played by others (especially those better than I am), and to read about its history and traditions. Those who have never played the game might find it difficult to understand or to appreciate the passion that golf can inspire in people who do play, but everyone who has played for any length of time has experienced that feeling. There simply is no other game like it.

I have been playing golf since I was about fourteen, and I have become convinced over time that this sometimes devilishly upsetting game is also the most spiritual one. If this seems paradoxical, all the better. Spirituality begins at the front door of mystery and seeks to open that door, even if just a crack. Any spirituality worth the name must allow for paradox, opposing extremes, and the admission that the mystery will never be penetrated fully.

I have a good friend who thinks that the connection between golf and the spiritual life is a stretch. And he has a point, I suppose. I do not think, for example, that a person needs only a set of clubs and a tee time in order to reach enlightenment. And I don't believe that proficiency in golf is synonymous with spiritual advancement. If that were true, then Jack Nicklaus, easily the best player of this century, would also be the most spiritually aware person of his time. Maybe he is. Everything I've read about him indicates that he is as gracious and generous as he is capable of playing the game. But I'd probably have to give the nod to someone like the Dalai Lama, and *he* plays to a twenty-six handicap.

So I'm not trying to turn golf into some kind of religion (lots of people have already tried that anyway). Instead, I'd say that if we apply the lessons that golf can teach to life in general, we will find that much of what we have learned can help us catch glimpses of the deeper life for which all human beings yearn. In other words, golf, like many human activities, has the potential for putting people in touch with the mystery that lies just beneath the surface of their lives. It takes some work, and the proper perspective, but the opportunities are there if a person is willing to look for them.

But I'm not suggesting that everyone take up golf. Most human endeavors can provide some spiritual insight, and it's already difficult enough to get a tee time. In fact, weekend play at some courses is so slow that all we're likely to learn is our capacity for murderous (or at least unkind) thoughts about the members of the foursome just ahead. While such musings might occupy the time between shots, they would probably have a deleterious effect on one's spiritual progress.

Anyone who is more than a casual golfer (if such an animal exists at all) has come face to face with paradox, seeming contradiction, and mystery plenty of times. A twenty handicap can scrape the ball around all afternoon and then sink an impossible fifteen foot sidehill putt on the eighteenth green to beat a player with a five handicap. The perfect drive can come to rest in a divot, while the errant shot may very well bounce off a tree and on to the green. Think of those little guys on tour who can hit the ball farther than Mario Lemieux or Mark Messier (I like hockey, too).

Such events occur in other games as well, but they are usually notable because they are also anomalous. When a slap shot off the stick of a big money player ricochets off the post, a dribbler from the third line defenseman may eventually ice the game in overtime. Everyone who follows football is aware of the miraculous pass known as the "immaculate reception," and basketball, baseball, and other sports have similar stories. But such events in other games are recalled because they are rarities. In golf, stories of this sort are commonplace, and everyone from the touring pro to the occasional golfer knows it. Other games may sometimes bring a player or fan face-to-face with analogies to a deeper, more spiritual life. Golf can't help but do it, and on a regular basis.

This is one piece of evidence which indicates that golf, like no other game, presents a player with countless opportunities to encounter mystery, to explore truths that are usually hidden beneath the busy-ness and complexities of modern life. Some of the lessons may be difficult to accept, but golf doesn't force a person to absorb them. The game simply presents the opportunities. A person can play golf all of her life and miss every new possibility that appears, but if she is patient and alert, she can learn a lot about herself and about the mystery that surrounds her. She might even have some fun, too, although enjoyment, alas, is not guaranteed. After all, some spiritual lessons are painful.

On the other hand, everyone knows the old saying that even the worst player in the world is likely to hit one shot in a round that will bring him back to the course again. It may be a good drive, a miraculous chip shot, or an approach that fades (intentionally or not) around a tree and finds its way to the green. Regardless, such experiences can inspire hope in the midst of despair, and can convince a person, despite a preponderance of evidence, that he *can* play the game, that he has what it takes to achieve a measure of success, as Jack Nicklaus likes to say. Golf tends to lure a

person back, just as the mystery that surrounds us constantly tries to get our attention.

The parallels to the rest of life are obvious. Sometimes,
even Scrooge finds that compassion, hitherto sneered at, has
its allure. Sometimes, the executive driven to succeed at all
costs becomes transfixed by the beauty of an autumn sunset.
From time to time, even when we are not looking for it, the
door opens a crack and mystery makes an appearance.

In our country, at least, people like to talk about sport as
a metaphor for life. While I suppose that this can be done
legitimately (even though some fans and sportscasters get it
backward), most of the analogies refer to democratic ideals
or utilitarian philosophies rather than to spiritual truths.
Democracy is fine by me, but it often fails to take into
account some of the deeper realities that spirituality takes
pains to acknowledge.

For example, common wisdom holds that under certain
circumstances, a baseball player should allow himself to be
struck by a pitch, to take one for the team, because the good
of the group is a higher value than that of the individual. In
other words, sports teach lessons about team play, about
being part of something bigger than oneself. While it is true
that people who live together must sometimes bow to the
will of the majority, this is not a spiritual absolute, because
spirituality proclaims the value, integrity, and uniqueness of
the individual. The needs of the individual can easily be lost
in the rush to satisfy the desires of the group. Spirituality,
unlike utilitarian philosophies, demands that the value of
the individual always be protected and even celebrated as
the principal means of achieving the greater good.

Beyond that, sports metaphors are ambiguous, at best.
Football, for example, can just as easily be an image for gang
violence as for democratic ideals. Tennis has too few variables. Baseball, though it can be intensely spiritual, is a team
game and cannot escape the inevitable references to the
good of the whole. Basketball and hockey are fun to watch

and to play (as long as you don't care much what happens to you), but they are team games. While I wouldn't rule out the possibility of gaining spiritual insight from these games, such insights must fight their way through a lot of clichés if they are going to benefit the participants or viewers spiritually. But no one can play even a casual round of golf without being presented with a few opportunities to encounter mystery and spiritual truth.

One of the more painful truths about human beings, however, is that we are slow learners, especially when we are confronted with mystery. We might convince ourselves that we have life and its mysteries figured out, only to take a fall and realize that we are back where we began. Or we may point out a fault in another without noticing that we too have that fault. We can even understand the spiritual benefits of golf and still pay mere lip service to them. We all talk a good game, but we often falter when we need to play it as it lies, on the course or at home. What we bring to the game (or to a church service, for that matter) can obscure the potential benefits that might be gained from the experience.

I know a man who, before he was married, told his fiancee that golf was the most important thing in his life. If she wanted their marriage to succeed (as if it were all up to her), she would do well to keep that in mind. He might be credited with honesty, at least, but it is clear that he was giving much more homage to the game than it deserved. Whether he knew it or not, he was asking more of the game than it could possibly give him. I would say that he had made golf into his religion, and that his worship got in the way of his ever gaining spiritual insight. The same thing happens when people make actual religion into their god.

Such an obsession with golf is so prevalent that many jokes are made about it. There's the one about the man who holds his hat over his heart as a funeral procession passes by the course. One of his playing companions takes this gesture as a sign of uncommon reverence until another player points out that the hearse contains the remains of the first man's wife. Many people who have taken up the game have faced the temptation to allow golf to dominate their lives, and everyone who plays knows someone who has given in to the temptation. Such an obsession becomes a substitute for true spirituality, just as religion (in its more unfortunate manifestations) can become the god that people worship. Golf can't guarantee spiritual insight any more than religion can. Yet both can lead people to deeper, ineffable truths, as long as they don't confuse means and ends.

I don't want to go on record as saying that golf and religion have the same value, of course. It's just that golf, like any human activity, can be an image of the spiritual life; and golf provides a better image than a lot of activities I can think of. Maybe that's why so many golf jokes involve the Persons of the Trinity and biblical figures like Moses and Saint Peter. Other sports generate anecdotes. Their stories celebrate famous plays and the people who made them, but jokes about those games do not abound because (in a general sense) what you see is what you get. In golf, there is always something more going on than the eye catches, and jokes that involve divine and saintly persons help people to get a glimpse of what is happening just below the surface.

It's still easy to ignore or otherwise to miss this, as obsessed golfers demonstrate, but missing the opportunities doesn't mean that they don't exist. Even though the spiritual lessons of golf are more difficult to ignore, a lot of players manage to squander them anyway. And obsessed golfers are not the only ones who run the risk of being blind to the spiritual qualities of the game. In fact, being good at golf is no guarantee of deepening one's appreciation of mystery. Because golf is the game it is, a duffer may very well reap every spiritual benefit which comes his way, while a scratch player may be so intent on scoring that he misses even the most obvious gift.

The attitudes we bring to the course can minimize golf's

impact upon us. Take, for example, the elitism that often threatens to poison the game. When the PGA finally got around to insisting that clubs that hosted tour events have an open membership policy, some few clubs decided to remain all white or all male or all Christian rather than change their ways. Some took one step forward by admitting black members, but then took it right back by remaining closed to women. Golf insists that everyone should be treated the same, yet people who are devoted to the game can miss the point by leaving fairness on the eighteenth green when they finish a round. We are all, indeed, slow learners.

Another friend tells me that he will eventually take up golf, when he doesn't have the energy for "real" sports. He's a racquetball player, and a good one, and I suppose that he likes to needle me because golf appears to be a game which anyone, in any condition, can play, whereas it takes a real man or woman to play "more active" games. But he has never played golf, so he doesn't appreciate the many challenges which the game presents. Beyond that, he doesn't realize that golf is the most spiritually rewarding of games in part because a person can play it and reap the benefits well into old age. Gene Sarazen played just about every day well into his eighties. Most people have to give up other sports long before that. It's remarkable that golf gives the possibility of great spiritual insight, and it's even more wondrous that the game can continue to do so as long as the player can get out to the course.

The point of all of this is that games, like other human activities, can occasionally provide the participant or the spectator with an inkling that there is more going on than meets the eye. This is all well and good, because getting in touch with mystery is the primary aim of human life and because everything we do has the potential to help us along the path. But among human recreational activities, golf is one game that cannot help but evoke the spiritual. The more we understand this, the better able we are to recognize and accept what the game has to offer.

So the intent of this book is to take a closer look at golf, a sport which is deeply individual, but which takes into account both fellow competitors and traditions. The player engages the game itself, rather than the opponent. And though one ever-present aim is to win, the person who plays golf stands to learn more about herself, to appreciate her fellow competitor, and to understand more about the presence of mystery in life. Above all else, the golfer has the opportunity to learn that life isn't about winning at all (though occasional successes are sweet); it's about discovering and then getting in synch with the rhythms of mystery.

1

APPROACH

I didn't know it at the time, but this book was conceived on an oppressively hot and humid August afternoon in 1988. As so often happens with conception, it was an accident; coming up with an idea for a book was the furthest thing from my mind. Before I knew it, however, the idea existed, and it would not die.

I was playing golf that August day, and I was playing miserably. My frustration was particularly intense, because I had played very well the previous week. On this day, however, I could do nothing right. When I was on the fifteenth tee, I hit the worst drive of the day, a dribbler that barely made it to the ladies' tee markers. In a moment of despair and anger, I quickly teed up another ball, barely took time to address it, and swung, without thinking at all.

It was the best drive I had ever hit. The ball rocketed off the tee, heading down the right-center portion of the fairway, then began to draw ever so slightly, finally landing in the middle of the fairway and rolling forever. When I got to the ball, I had a nine iron left to the green on a par four of about 400 yards.

My playing partners were impressed, and I tried to act as if this sort of thing happened all of the time, but my mind and my emotions were racing to make sense out of what had taken place. I was so intent on repeating the phenomenon that I chili-dipped my short iron. Eventually, I took a six on the hole. That, at least, was a familiar experience.

I had always wanted to hit the ball like that, and I believed that I could learn to do so. But once it happened, I was faced with several dilemmas. In the first place, I did not know how I had managed to do it. I knew that it had felt terrific, but I was *certain* that I couldn't recreate the swing that had produced such a wonderful shot.

Two things were clear to me. First, I had swung without going through my preshot routine (nowadays *everybody* has one), and I had not consulted the extensive checklist that usually clutters my head as I stand over the ball. I had simply swung, but because I was angry and frustrated, I felt that I had just been going through the motions. I didn't care where the damned ball went.

Even more perplexing was the sensation I had when I finished the swing and spied the ball as it raced away from me down the fairway. As I hit the ball, I had the distinct impression that it wouldn't go very far because I wasn't exerting the force I usually apply. It *felt* as if I had swung lazily, but the length of the drive told me that I had brought a lot of force to bear.

My customary swing was a confused jumble of arms and legs, as I tried to hit the ball as hard as I possibly could. The theory was that making a ball at rest go a great distance required a lot of muscle and effort. And it didn't matter that I rarely hit the ball that far. If a shot only carried half as far as it should have, I had only swung half as hard as I needed to. In the world I inhabited, this passed for common sense. You can imagine how violent my swing could sometimes get.

Now I had hit the shot of my life, without feeling as if I had used much force at all. I had, of course, suddenly and accidentally stumbled upon rhythm and tempo. It was a new experience, and I liked it, but, as I said, I had no clue how to recreate it.

Because I had experienced it, however, I suddenly knew

that becoming a good player had less to do with sheer force and more to do with timing. It was one of those classic demonstrations of the principle that less is more. It occurred to me that I had been approaching the game incorrectly all those years I had been trying to play it. Unfortunately, despite the evidence of the shot I had hit, I wasn't sure that I could develop into the player I'd always wanted to be. It's one thing to stumble upon a good swing; it's quite another to be able to recreate it whenever you want to.

On that afternoon, I got a brief look at something elusive. Life provides us with plenty of opportunities to be confused or unsure about why or how something or other has happened. More often than not, our thoughts and feelings race to catch up with something that is just beyond our grasp. But then, every so often, we have a moment of clarity when everything comes together. Grateful as we are for these moments, we wonder if we can find ways to retain that clarity.

As I walked toward the next tee that afternoon, I forgot about golf entirely and found myself remembering an occasion several years before. As part of my seminary training, I had been required to spend a semester taking a course in pastoral theology called Clinical Pastoral Education. My training took place at Northwestern Memorial Hospital in Chicago.

It was (and is) an immense place, very intimidating to a boy from Nashville. When I found out that I was expected to spend several nights that summer as the only chaplain in the hospital, I became a bit anxious. When the first evening came, I was in a panic.

What terrible situations were going to occur that evening? What horrors was I going to have to deal with? What would I do if I were confronted with the parents of a child killed in an accident? I imagined a thousand horrible scenarios, most of which I was sure would play themselves out before morning. The first time my beeper went off, my heart instantly jumped to my throat. As I hurried toward the emergency room, I was trying to remember all of the comforting thoughts and gestures in my arsenal. I was flailing, my usual response to stressful situations. It felt a lot like standing on the first tee of a new and unfamiliar course with the entire world watching on television.

In the face of this stressful situation, I decided to do what I had always done. I geared up to concentrate on the strength that I believed I needed. As I thought about it, I realized that I actually had quite a bit of ammunition. After all, I had been in the seminary for two years by then, and I had learned all sorts of useful things. The Scripture and theology courses gave me many possible approaches. I even knew a few words of Greek, though I wasn't sure how I could get the conversation to turn in directions that would allow me to use them. But no matter; I was armed to the teeth, and I was going to make everything better for the people who were waiting for me. I was, in short, ready to swing away.

The emergency room was filled with people, most of whom turned out to be relatives and friends of a boy who had been shot. This was truly as bad as any of the tragedies I had imagined. All of the boy's sisters and brothers were crying and alternately pacing around the room and throwing themselves into each other's arms or onto the nearest chair. His parents were surrounded by well-meaning friends, some of whom were plotting revenge against the person who had done the shooting. It was a confused mess, and I had no idea where to start. Despite (and perhaps because of) all of my theological training, I was at a loss.

Faced with this confusion, I forgot all of my lines, all of my strategies for dispensing comfort. My mind went blank. But I knew I was expected to do *something*. So I walked over to the parents, introduced myself, and asked them if there was anything I could do for them.

Even as I said this, I thought it sounded pretty weak. I

was sure that my words would be ineffective. But the parents' reaction surprised me. It turned out that there were quite a few things I could do for them. They had thus far been unable to find out anything about their son's condition, and they wanted to know if there was a quiet place where they and their children could gather. After I had done this for them, they asked me if I would pray with them, and I found that the words came easily. I was a calm presence in the midst of a stormy and confusing time. I found that the less I struggled for the "right" thing to say, the more I found myself saying what the family needed to hear. In other words, the less force I tried to generate, the more effective my actions became.

I hadn't thought about that family for years, but they popped into my mind that afternoon on the golf course. That's when I realized that I had experienced many of the same feelings when I hit that wonderful drive. I had done what came naturally, I hadn't tried to force anything. I had exerted no effort at all (at least compared to my customary swing), and the result was beyond my imagining. For the first time, I sensed a connection between my approaches to golf and to life in general.

This shouldn't have surprised me. Anyone who believes in God knows that access to the mysteries of life can only come through the people and events around us. What we can see helps us to understand that which we cannot see. And faith, in turn, helps us to interpret the events of our lives and to come to deeper understandings of ourselves and other people. For people of faith, God can be present on the golf course as easily as in a chapel. It's all a matter of perspective.

In other words, we can all use what is familiar to us as a means of gaining insight into the mysteries of God and human life. If we look closely at the events of our lives, we can find ourselves understanding those mysteries as never before.

When we do this, the familiar becomes an image by

which we understand that which is beyond our comprehension. For example, none of the poetry in the world can unlock all of the mysteries of love, but it can get us in the door. Love may remain ultimately beyond our ability to comprehend, but poetry helps us to know when it's in the neighborhood. Love remains a mystery, but it's a mystery which we can see in action.

On that August afternoon, when I hit an uncharacteristically good drive and then thought about the family I met in the emergency room, I began to understand that golf is a particularly apt metaphor for the spiritual life. People who are not familiar with the game may not understand this, but those of us who play the game are aware, on some level, that this is true. There is no magic about it. Poor golfers can become spiritually advanced, and pros can ignore the presence of mystery, even when it hits them with the force of a full five iron. Ability doesn't necessarily affect insight. But just as high handicappers could become better players if they paid attention to some of the subtleties of the game, anyone can become more spiritually aware by treating golf as an image of the spiritual life.

I had always *known*, for example, that rhythm and tempo are far more important to the golf swing than sheer power. But on that August afternoon, I *experienced* it as truth. Prior to that day, I had always allowed my feeling that I had to swing as if my life depended upon it to overwhelm and obscure what I knew, namely, that power comes from a smooth blending of moving parts rather than sheer force. In the same way, when I walked into that emergency room and was so overwhelmed by the enormity of the chaos, I found that I was indeed helpful to that family precisely because I simply presented myself to them and let them set the agenda. They knew, far better than I, what they needed. And they got what they needed because I didn't try to force some abstract theology on them.

Golf is full of little lessons like that, examples that people can apply to their lives in ways that present them with opportunities to grow spiritually, to become more aware of the presence of mystery as it appears in and around the events of their lives. Sometimes, as on that afternoon on the course, mystery jumps right up in front of us; at other times, it is subtler, and easy to miss. Regardless, when we look at golf as an image of the spiritual journey, we might accomplish much more than an improvement in our scores. We might learn that a balance between what we think and what we feel puts us in the presence of mystery. When we are only thinking or only feeling, we tend to let mystery slip right past us.

Several years ago, I was working on the best round of golf of my life. As I approached the sixteenth tee, I was only three over par. Even if I bogeyed the last three holes, I would surpass my previous best by one shot. Anyone who plays golf can appreciate my excitement. Non-golfers could get an idea of what this meant to me if they recalled the happiest moment of their lives and multiplied the feeling by four.

On this course, sixteen was a par four, dogleg right around a small lake. Unfortunately, I hit my drive to the right. Though I was not in the rough or the water, I would have to carry the approach over the water to reach the green. I didn't think that this presented me with much of a problem, however. The day had been going so well that I decided to play a fade. This would allow me to reach the green in two despite the obstacle that the water presented.

Why didn't I simply hit over the lake? Well, I was working on the best round of my life, and I didn't want to take any chances. Water and I had never gotten along that well. I almost drowned once, and knowing the feeling, I didn't want to subject my golf ball to such terrors. Plus, having to hit over water brought back numerous memories of failure, and I wanted to have only positive thoughts as I stood over

the ball. I was congratulating myself for this line of thinking as I lined up the shot. As it turned out, I wasn't thinking at all.

Since I wanted to have only happy thoughts at this time,
I considered that players hit fades all of the time. Any pro
(with the possible exception of Bruce Lietzke) can play
either a fade or a draw, depending on the circumstances.
And a lot of good players (including Bruce Lietzke) routinely play from left to right. If they could do it, then I saw no
reason why I couldn't. In fact, I was sure that I could do it.

But this feeling was competing with an opposing one.
Although I had hit the ball from left to right many times in
my golfing life, and many of these shots had been rather
extreme fades (slices, if I'm being honest), it occurred to me
that I had never once hit a fade *on purpose*. I could only play
a fade if I had no idea that I was doing it. As I began my
backswing, this feeling crowded out the confident one I had
been experiencing as I first addressed the ball.

This proved to be a fatal mistake. I hit the ball dead
straight, and it went a long way, over the trees to the left of
the fairway and out of bounds. I was so disgusted with the
result that I dropped another ball (careful to extend my arm
fully before taking the drop), set up and hit it again, with
the same result.

As I put the number nine on my scorecard, a song began
to play in my head, which was just as well, because there was
no point in thinking about setting a new personal scoring
record. In fact, I was so distracted by the disaster that I put
two more high numbers on the card for seventeen and eighteen. The score I eventually posted didn't even break into
my personal top ten.

The Beatles song was still playing in my head (number
nine, number nine) as I walked to my car, and I was tempted
to write a nasty letter to Yoko Ono, but then I found myself
recounting the debacle on number sixteen. It was clear to me
that the memory, like the ball, was not going to fade.

I *could* have done it differently. Had I played with even a hint of caution, I'd have hit a short iron over a corner of the lake and then hit another one onto the green. At the time, however, that felt way too puny to me. After all, I was having the round of my life. I saw no reason why I couldn't pull off a specialized shot, considering how things had been going. I actually felt certain that I could pull it off, that I could work my will and do what I had never done before. Only after the fact did I realize I was reaching beyond my grasp.

This is exactly the sort of hubris that got Oedipus, Macbeth, and the rest of that crowd into trouble. While my experience was not quite on a par (sorry about that) with theirs, it was similar. Like them, I couldn't simply let things unfold; I had to force the issue. And, like them, just as I could see the prize before me, it disappeared from view, beyond a barbed wire fence, and I was left with nothing. How very tragic it all was.

Anyone with half a brain could have told me that the pros spend years practicing how to fade or draw the ball at will, and even they sometimes fail to accomplish what they have in mind. When they try something fancy, they have at least a reasonable expectation of success because they have practiced it beforehand. And the truth is that they will often play things a bit safer, preferring to aim for the center of the green, for example, rather than trying to force the ball into a precarious pin position.

I wasn't thinking about any of that as I mapped out my strategy. I was sure that I could do anything, because the round had been going so well. In the end, however, the realization that I didn't know how purposely to fade the ball set in as I was swinging, and my confidence disappeared, only to be replaced with yet another certainty: that I was going to shoot myself in the foot.

Earlier in the same round, I had decided to putt the ball through a lengthy patch of fringe, because I was more confident putting than chipping. I almost holed the putt, and I saved par by choosing wisely. At the time, I didn't think to congratulate myself for "staying within myself," as they say, probably because the result was a good one. Had I been thinking the same way on sixteen, I'd have planned a different strategy. The result might well have been another par. Regardless, I would probably have taken nine out of play by choosing to hit two short irons instead of one five iron fade. Why didn't I stick with what I knew?

It's a good question, and there are many possible answers. In general, I suppose that I let my emotions get the better of me. When I could see that great score right in front of me, I allowed my excitement to veto any input from my brain. My brain told me that I didn't know how to play a fade, but my feelings told me that this was irrelevant. When my brain suggested a short iron over the edge of the lake, my emotions told me that this was far too cowardly for a player of my expertise. And so on. The feelings convinced me to try the shot, but they didn't have the power to help me pull it off. And my feelings did not bother to tell me this until I was in the middle of my backswing.

Unquestioned feelings tend to become extreme, and that's when people find themselves in trouble. Anger becomes rage, guilt becomes shame, and so on. This is why human beings were created with brains, not to shut the feelings down, but to determine whether or not the feelings are valid. Sometimes, for example, I *feel* guilty even though I have done nothing wrong. If I let my brain join the internal monologue that drones inside me, I just might figure out that I can choose to lay the guilt aside, since I am blameless for now.

This is a little drill that I have only recently learned. But if I had been alert, I could have picked it up on the golf course years ago. The game presents people with countless opportunities to allow their thoughts and feelings to engage in dialogue. Had I granted my brain equal time, I'd have toned down the excitement which led me to believe I could do what I had never done before. My trying to play a fade wasn't even a calculated risk (which good players take from time to time); it was foolishness, pure and simple. And as is often the case, the foolishness was inspired by unquestioned, extreme, and faulty feelings.

Sometimes, we have to go with what the gut tells us, but we are generally better off, on the course and elsewhere, if we get the thoughts and feelings talking with each other. In the absence of this balance, we get ourselves into all sorts of unnecessary trouble. We succumb to the lure of certainty, and we only realize our mistake after that certainty has seduced us into reaching beyond our grasp. When our thinking and feeling are balanced, we become less certain, but, paradoxically, we perform better because we are including more variables. Failure to balance thoughts and feelings leads us to ignore the variables, to act as if they did not exist or did not contain any useful information.

I suppose that I deserve points or something for this, but I've only thrown a golf club once in my life. It was a five iron, and it sailed a lot farther than the ball I had just attempted to hit. Interestingly enough, the technique I used to throw it was pretty close to the one I *should* have been using in my swing, but that's another story. I'd been playing for many years by the time I pitched that five iron, but the temptation to throw a club appeared early in my golfing life. The first time I ever played, in fact, I became so frustrated that I considered, at several points during the nine hole round, at least *tossing* a club or two (I was ignorant of golf etiquette in this regard at the time).

The game looks so easy when you see someone else play it. If you are lucky enough to watch a good player swing a club and to see the ball disappear into the ozone, you get a glimpse of what a joy the game can sometimes be. If, on the other hand, you watch a poorer player hit the ball badly, you might be tempted, as I was, to think that you can do much better than he has done. After all, the ball just sits there. It's not as if people were throwing it at you, adding a nasty spin like they do in baseball. And it's not as if you are sitting atop a moving horse, as is the case in polo, when you are trying to advance the ball.

What could be simpler? You stand still over a ball that is not moving, and you take as much time as you want (at least if you're one of several particularly slow tour players). It stands to reason that you should be able to hit the ball passably well at least every other time or two. But, as everyone who knows the game can tell you, it isn't nearly as simple as that. As I said, I'd been playing for years when I first threw a club. By that time, I *knew* how sneakily difficult the game is, but that didn't stop me. Despite what I knew, I *felt* that I should have been able to do it right just about every time. An ever-widening gulf between what a player knows and what he feels is a constant danger in golf. And when knowing and feeling are at odds, all sorts of bad things may happen.

I once witnessed a playing partner's tantrum that ended with his throwing all of his equipment into a conveniently placed lake (into which his ball had disappeared only seconds before). He was having a particularly bad day, but even so, his tirade was unexpected. Usually the most gentle of people, he was always fun to play golf with because of his self-deprecating humor. If he hit a bad shot, he was sure to come out with a comment that cracked the rest of us up. Though he was a fine athlete, success at golf had always eluded him, but no one thought that this bothered him. His comments seemed to indicate that he enjoyed himself despite his poor play.

Then he threw his clubs into the lake, and all of us had to adjust our opinions of his relationship with golf. It didn't take long. After all, the rest of us knew what he was feeling because we had felt it ourselves. This supposedly simple game, this game that we all played whenever we had the time, this game whose mysteries had always eluded us, was under our skin, and it ached terribly, like a disease whose cause and cure were beyond medical science. Sometimes, the disease erupted violently; we all knew the symptoms.

The disease sometimes appears when all practice swings are perfect but all real attempts to hit the ball look like the moves of a hyperactive contortionist. Sometimes, the outbreak follows a perfect drive and a shanked wedge. Some people lose it when their playing companion's ball bounces off a tree into the fairway and their own drive hits the same tree and stays in the branches. What's been simmering beneath the surface erupts: some players get quiet, some throw clubs, and some begin to hit shots without really getting set or going through a routine. And all of this is brought about by one unvarying factor.

It's that gulf between knowing and feeling. Every player knows that golf is perhaps the most difficult of games, despite what it looks like. Yet all of us who play it feel that we should be better than we are. This is what caused our companion's explosion that afternoon. He knew he was playing a difficult game, but he felt that he should be playing it well. When the debate within him got heated enough, his *thought* that the game was difficult was overwhelmed by the *feeling* that, difficult or not, he should have figured it out by now. As soon as the feeling outweighed the thought, he threw his stuff into the lake. Then he stomped off the course, vowing never to play the stupid (actually, his language was more colorful) game again.

We all knew how he felt. Even if we hadn't thrown so much as a broken tee during our playing lives, we'd been tempted to. Golf does that to people. If it didn't look so easy, perhaps we'd be better able to control our feelings. As it is, however, the ball still sits there, daring us to hit it capably. And we fail a lot more often than we succeed. Even as we walk up to a well-hit drive, we believe that we are supposed to be able to duplicate the feat and reach the green in regulation. And the ball sits there again, sometimes even smiling up at us with a look that says, "I bet you can't do that again."

A few weeks later, our equipment-throwing friend called me to see if I wanted to play a quick nine. I almost didn't know what to say. After all, his clubs were still at the bottom of that lake. But then he told me that he had a new set of clubs. "I'm just dying to try them out," he said. It was as if his old set of clubs had simply worn out from being hit so consistently on the sweet spot. Of *course* he had a new set of clubs. It was the most natural thing in the world, wasn't it?

So I agreed to play with him, and I never mentioned the old set of clubs, even when he hit the new ones as poorly as he had the old. I didn't say anything because, though I had never thrown even one club into a lake, I had, on several occasions, vowed that I would never play the game again. A couple of times, I had even said this loudly enough for my friends to hear, and they had never said anything about it when I called them a few days or weeks later. One day, I quit the game after a terrible round in the morning and was at the practice range a little after five that evening. But I digress.

One day, long after our friend buried his clubs at sea, and after I had been playing for years, I threw that five iron. As it sailed through the air, a strange thought came to me. I always told myself that I played golf "for fun," but that was obviously not the case. Had I been playing for fun, I'd never have thrown the club. Had my friend been playing for fun, he'd never have thrown all of his equipment into the lake. Had any of us played the game for fun, we'd never have gone through the routine of quitting one moment and taking it up again the next.

Our problem, I think, was that we all approached the game as human beings tend to approach life in general. Whether we are on the course, at our jobs, or with our friends and families, we pay little attention to the disparity between our thoughts and feelings until one of them over-whelms the other. That's when the explosions of despair or anger or shame occur. Then the clubs fly, or the cruel words pass our lips, or we run out of the house, vowing revenge.

One of golf's great gifts to people is the clear message that it's important to reconcile what we feel and what we think. We may very well know that the game is difficult, but as long as we feel that we should master it, the disappoint-ments and explosions are bound to occur from time to time. It's only when we allow what we know to influence what we feel that we begin to achieve a balance that will allow us to accept both the failures and the triumphs as part of the game. This balance also presents us with the opportunity to put the good and bad into perspective.

On any weekend, we can see the professionals do this. Some are better than others, but none of them would be there unless they could allow their thoughts to influence their feelings and their feelings to influence their thoughts. You can see this each time a player who is on a tear choos-es one club less because he is pumped up, or when a guy who has just taken double bogey pulls himself together and birdies the next hole. You can see it when a player who is in contention makes an incredibly creative shot when logic would dictate that he is dead where he stands.

This is why golf, more than any other sport, is a mirror for life lived creatively and spiritually. As difficult as it is to balance what we know and what we feel on the course, it's considerably easier than it is in the other areas of our lives. We have to start somewhere; it might as well be on the first tee.

What we can learn about the balance between knowing and feeling can help us to lessen the influence of any num-ber of deadly beliefs, one of the most painful of which is the one that convinces us we have to be perfect to be worth-while at all.

All human beings are overwhelmed by such feelings at

one time or another, and although the feelings are often fueled by the expectations of others, we also manage to create the expectation all by ourselves. It's a feeling of being less than we believe we should be which drives us to seek perfection as the only acceptable option. And, of course, the more we feel this, the greater the stakes become and the more magnified our mistakes appear to us. Pretty soon, we find ourselves alternating between feverish attempts to reach perfection and the desire to stop trying completely. What's worse is that each triumph actually increases the pressure to perform at least as well the next time.

A person's spirit can be crushed beneath such expectations, whether they originate inside him or are imposed from without and accepted as valid. The desire for perfection is composed of unquestioned feelings of fear and shame, and it becomes a never-ending downward spiral. Nothing is ever enough to satisfy the feelings for long, and even a ninety-nine on a test may feel like failure because, good as it is, it isn't the perfection the person believes he needs.

Though I've never taken a poll about this, I'd bet that the majority of people who take up golf have a secret desire for perfection, a sincerely held belief that perfection can be reached. And such people see a lack of perfection as evidence that they've failed to figure it out yet. For perfectionists, golf is more painful than enjoyable because it looks so easy but is really so difficult. They keep coming back, hoping to find the key, but over time, the game slowly teaches them a lesson they never sought to learn.

It took me forever to understand that golf had offered me, from the moment I took it up, an antidote to the belief that I was supposed to be perfect. But I missed the point of all those years because I didn't know how to balance the thoughts and feelings I carried around. This does not make me unique, however. We're all slow learners, remember?

Because none of us are quick studies in spiritual matters,

we will always do battle with thoughts and feelings, both on the course and off. But golf can help us to nurture the dialogue between knowing and thinking. This is vital, because mystery becomes visible whenever thoughts and feelings intersect.

What we learn on the course can help us in other parts of our lives, if we take it home with us. We might learn sooner rather than later that perfection is unattainable, that playing poorly today doesn't eliminate the possibility of doing better the next time out, that making a mistake disciplining our children doesn't make us bad parents. Even Nicklaus and the Dalai Lama have their bad days, but you don't see them throwing up their hands and saying nasty things to themselves. Even if they do, they quickly get themselves back into balance. We should all be so good at it.

2

PLAYING IT AS IT LIES

My regular playing partners and I have an understanding. We agree on the rules. This does not mean, however, that we follow all the rules of golf as they are written. Instead, we have all come to accept that certain rules may be broken on a regular basis. These infractions have become so routine that no one questions them any more.

I should be surprised that we can do this without a twinge of guilt or protest. I certainly remember my sandlot days, when no one was allowed to get away with a violation of the rules (at least without a fight). And when we played football (tackle, of course) on Sundays during high school, we all did our best to play by the rules; if there was a dispute, it always centered around an infraction of some sort. Did the defender interfere with the pass receiver or not? Even though these disputes could be bitter, they arose because we all believed that rules should be followed.

But my golfing partners and I pass right over that little consideration, at least in certain areas. We always play "winter rules," even when it's hot enough for us to play shirtless. Thus, everyone is entitled to roll the ball in the fairway (and in the rough, too). If we were asked, I suppose we'd say that this practice grew out of the understanding that the course we usually play is only sporadically maintained, and that it is, therefore, often difficult to get a nice, tight lie even in the fairway a good bit of the time. But the practice has become so accepted that, even on the rare occasions when we visit a really nice course, the same rule applies.

I'd be ashamed to admit this, except that it is an almost universally accepted way of doing things. At least when rank amateurs get together to play, it seems that everyone rolls the ball, "just a little." Even when this is the usual practice, the rule can become a bit hazy. How far may a person actually move his ball? Is it permissible to find the nearest patch of good grass (in the fairway), and may a player whose ball is in the rough place the ball on a nice lie, even though it had been so deeply buried that it took five minutes to find it? These metaphysical questions always arise.

As is the case in every area of life, once you begin to ignore the truth, you find that you have strayed far from it. Since our "rule" is so slippery, a player may find a way to justify any improvement of a lie. If, for example, I can roll my ball in the rough, then why am I not allowed to move a ball with a good lie so that I can avoid an overhanging branch? The answer is that there is no reason not to give myself relief (notice the use of good golf terminology), since I give myself relief all of the time anyway. The term relief is appropriate here, if for no other reason than to demonstrate how easily we can take a word that has legitimate uses and mangle it until it means whatever we wish it to mean.

You'd think that this casual attitude toward playing the ball as it lies makes everyone happy, but I think we all retain a secret gripe or two. At least one time a round, an observer could tell by the look on a player's face that someone has taken more "relief" than he is entitled to. After all, this is a friendly game, and everyone should strive to take about as much advantage as everyone else. But since it's a friendly game, no one ever speaks up to say, "Wait a minute. You moved your ball too far." Interestingly enough, no one ever accuses himself of doing this. It's always someone else who takes unfair advantage. Once again, relief, which has specific meaning in the context of the rules of the game, becomes a means of gaining unfair advantage or of resenting someone else who has done so.

We have other rules interpretations that wouldn't survive on the tour or at the club tournament, either. All of us consider a lost ball penalty enough. Because golf balls are expensive, we allow the player to drop and then to roll another ball with no additional penalty in the general area where he last saw his ball disappear. It will come as no surprise that the player always finds that he has a pretty good lie. And a lie it is, although none of us like to think about it that way. After all, this is a friendly game, and nothing of consequence is at stake, right? Golf is no different from any other area of life: a person always faces the temptation to delude himself, others, or both. And when people work at this together, they can learn to succumb to temptation on a regular basis.

Mulligans (one a side) are a regular feature as well. The accepted interpretation is that one can only be taken from the tee. But if someone is having a particularly bad day, the rest of us will encourage him to take another stab at a short putt that he has missed. We all congratulate ourselves on our caring natures when this occurs. If we thought about it a bit, however, we might realize that we are not being compassionate as much as we are conspiring to allow someone to avoid facing the truth, albeit in a small way.

We also consider it acceptable to take a "provisional" mulligan (again note the use of proper golf terminology). If my drive on a hole appears to have bounced into the woods, I may take another shot, but if I find my first ball on the edge of the fairway, I can pick up the mulligan and use it later. And because I am entitled to the mulligan, I can hit a second drive on number nine, even if my first shot looks good. I may really blast one, and I don't have to use the mulligan anyway (see the previous rule about "provisional" mulligan).

I could go on, because there are all sorts of rules that

apply to hazards (lateral and otherwise), spike marks, and so on. But I think that this cursory look at the rules my friends and I follow paints a full enough picture. In general, if we were asked, we'd say that we allow ourselves these breaks because we don't play golf for a living. It's supposed to be fun, and, as I said, the courses we play are not in the best of shape. Why spoil a potentially great time by being rigid about the rules? Life is too short to be so compulsive, right?

If our attempts at self-justification seem rather hollow, it's no surprise. When we tune in to a tournament on TV, we see people who play a very different game. On one occasion that I know of, Hale Irwin probably lost a chance to win the British Open because he counted a failed stab at a putt as a stroke, even though he might have gotten away with it by saying that he had, indeed, *started* to make a stroke but had decided to hold back at the last second.

My friends and I would never have counted it against him (and he had a lot more at stake than we ever do). We tend to give each other short putts, and it's such a common practice that we never say anything, even when a player gives himself a sidehill putt of three or four feet. If one of us backhands a short putt and misses it, someone else immediately says something like, "That was good," thus easing (even eliminating) his pain. We never think for long about eliminating the person's responsibility to play by the rules. After all, he'd give us the same break. This is a fine example of how honesty virtually disappears when groups conspire to let their members off the hook. It is so easily replaced by a collective decision to call black white and vice versa.

If we really thought about what we were doing, we'd probably change our ways. One of the elements that sets golf apart from every other game is its rules and the understanding that players are responsible for enforcing them. One needs very little additional evidence to conclude that golf is the most spiritual of games.

But my friends and I (and an awful lot of people)

squander many of the spiritual benefits because we play golf
as if it were some other sport whose rules are made to be
broken, at least on occasion. Since we don't play the game
for a living, and we are not trying to become number one in
the world (or on the block), it's easy for us to think that it's
no big deal to play by our own set of rules. We're only fool-
ing ourselves.

The high school where I used to teach had a golf tournament at the end of each year, and everyone played. One
teacher, a man who rarely played the game, had the habit of
bringing a counter to the course with him. He knew that he
was going to take a lot of strokes and he wanted to be accurate about his score. The device attached easily to his belt,
and each time that he made a pass at the ball, he reached for
the counter and clicked.

About midway through the round he hit a fairly good
drive, but the ball came to rest a few feet behind a tree.
When he hit his next shot, the ball rocketed back off the
tree and caught him dead center, about six inches below his
navel. He crumpled to the ground, and his playing companions rushed over to attend to him. But he insisted that he
was all right, and after a few minutes he got shakily to his
feet, dusted himself off, and reached for the counter on his
belt. He clicked it once and went off to retrieve his ball. We
should all be so honest.

But it's not just a matter of honesty, though that comes
into play; and it's not all that much about fair play, though
that is implied. Instead, if we were to follow the rules of
golf, accepting penalty strokes when they apply, and always
playing the ball as it lies, we would, in spiritual terms, also
be accepting responsibility for our actions. After all, the ball
didn't just magically find its way into the rough. We hit it
there. We would also be taking what life hands us and dealing with it as best we can, realizing that we sometimes get
good breaks even when we haven't done anything to deserve
them as well as bad ones when we are doing the best we can.

The way most people play golf indicates that they don't much appreciate the various twists of fate that occur in the rest of their lives. For example, if I hit a terrible shot and it bounces off a tree and back into the fairway, I'm more than happy to accept responsibility for it. It's only when I'm not satisfied with the shot that I look for ways to improve the lie.

Every time that I improve a lie, I'm really letting myself off the hook. It seems a harmless way to avoid facing the consequences of my actions, but the more I do it on the course, the more likely I am to justify similar actions everywhere else as well. Like most people, I was already finding ways to improve my lie before I ever picked up a club. I suspect that everyone learns to fudge a little, and this explains why golf instructors try to instill a respect for the rules in their students. They know that golf's rules can be an antidote for a careless disregard for honesty.

Since we are speaking of lies, it's probably appropriate to mention the "white" lies that everyone likes to get away with from time to time. While this can be viewed as a moral issue, I think that people's motivation for fudging the truth a bit has other implications. As often as not, we withhold the truth either because we wish to avoid the consequences of our actions or because we wish to "protect" people from a truth that we believe is too much for them. In either case, we are deluding ourselves and the people we lie to or allow to lie to us. We don't present ourselves to each other as we are, because we live out of a secret fear that we are somehow unacceptable unless we tweak the figures a bit. And we allow others to get away with less than the truth because we wish to spare them from the pain of falling short of our expectations of them (as if living up to our expectations were what life was all about).

It seems like such a little thing, on the course or in the living room, this telling of little lies. But the result is that we keep others from knowing us as we are and allow them to do the same. Pretty soon, nobody knows who anyone else is.

Each time I roll the ball in the fairway because I'm looking for the perfect lie, I am ignoring the opportunity to take life as it is and myself as I am. It's an indication that I don't really believe that I am acceptable as I am, or that I have to look for some kind of advantage just to level the playing field and make an impact. How did I ever get to this point?

The answer is that I got here one little lie at a time. If I had started playing golf by the rules, I might have caught myself at it a lot earlier. The game has some built in antidotes to self-delusion, and they can remind a player of the spiritual imperative to root out such delusions from his life as well as from his game. When we choose to ignore what golf has to offer, we lose the chance to apply what it teaches us to other parts of our lives.

If you need any evidence that golf, when it is played by the rules, is the most spiritual of games, you need look no further than the latest edition of ESPN's Sportscenter. The following fantasy broadcast should suffice:

> There were six seconds left, and the Bulls were down by one point. Everyone in the building expected Michael to get the ball, so there was some surprise when Rodman took the inbound pass and put up a hook shot. But Jordan came out of nowhere to tip the rebound back in. As the crowd roared its approval and the Bulls began to celebrate, however, Michael held up his hand for quiet. He walked to the scorer's table, took the microphone, and explained that he had touched the ball while it was still in the cylinder. The basket shouldn't have counted, he said, and the Bulls left the floor with a loss. Everyone complimented Michael on his tremendous sportsmanship.

This is preposterous on the face of it, as everyone knows. No one could expect a basketball player (even the sainted Michael) to be so precise in his adherence to rules of the game. If Deion Sanders stopped the game and insisted that he had actually interfered with the wide receiver, everyone would think that he had lost his mind. If Ken Griffey made what looked like a spectacular, shoestring catch and the umpire signaled "Out," he would be foolish to indicate in some way that he had really trapped it. He might gloat about it after the game, but he'd say nothing at the time. So what if the umpire missed the call? Those are the breaks of the game.

But golf is different. Most people who play the game know at least one story of a player who has lost a chance to win an important championship by calling a penalty on himself. I've already mentioned the one about Hale Irwin penalizing himself a stroke at the British Open. And anyone familiar with golf knows how Davis Love III made it into the Masters in 1995 by winning the tournament just the week before. Only a few also know that he'd already have been in had he fudged a little and not called a penalty on himself at a tournament the previous season.

Tournaments from the U.S. Open to the club championship have been lost by players who might have gotten by without penalizing themselves, but who decided to play by the rules. Even friendly matches at municipal courses are also sometimes decided on the basis of a penalty which a player calls on himself. Contrast that with the arguments on any playground about whether or not a runner beat a throw or about who fouled whom. Watch a friendly game of tennis (if there is such a thing) some time, and listen to the arguments about whether or not a shot landed in.

Golf is unique among sports in the way that players routinely penalize themselves, but the difference doesn't stop there. It pays to know the rules in any sport, but most sports are set up in such a way that breaking the rules on purpose is often the right thing to do.

If Wayne Gretzky is alone on a breakaway in overtime of

a playoff game, any player in the league will tell you that you should trip him, or slash him, or cross-check him (aren't hockey terms wonderful?), or do whatever comes into your head as long as it prevents him from taking a shot on goal. None of these things are legal, but hockey, like most games, doesn't bother to dwell on such niceties as rules when the game is on the line.

The object is to win, and if you can get away with a few rules violations along the way, so much the better. Anything that prevents or forestalls losing or gains an advantage is acceptable in most sports. This is such an integral part of sports that it is not even questioned. Of course players cheat. Everyone does. They're all looking for that advantage. People generally fail to mention this when they are proclaiming that sport is an apt metaphor for life.

This means that golf is either the dumbest sport ever invented, or the most sublime. If you've read this far, you know which answer I favor. If you think about it, other games, with their emphasis on winning at any cost, may be more like life as it is. After all, people didn't dream up sayings like "it's a dog-eat-dog world" because everyone always plays fair or considers the feelings of others on a regular basis. In business, or on the school yard, you have to play with the figures a little, don't you? You can't just tell the truth or play fair all of the time, at least not if you want to get ahead. Maybe this is why people like sports metaphors so much. They talk about team play and sacrificing yourself for the good of the others, and this seems like a good image for what should go on day to day. But they never mention the hand check or the thoroughbred whose blood is racing with an illegal drug or two. And they never, never mention golf.

Golf's rules, and the ways in which players adhere to them, make it a purer game. The game simply has no analogy to tripping Gretzky or applying a bit of saliva to the ball. In fact, golf could not exist as the game it is if players didn't scrupulously follow the rules and penalize themselves for violations. But it goes beyond that. Tom Kite once prevented someone from making a shot when he saw that the player would incur a penalty if he did not take a stance outside a marked area. He stopped him because he's a good guy, but also because he knew he'd have to assess a penalty on his playing companion if the shot had been made. Because he saw that there was a potential violation, he *had* to act, one way or another. He couldn't just turn away and pretend that he hadn't seen anything. That's golf.

At least that's golf as it is meant to be played. And this is why so many people miss the opportunities that golf provides them with when they routinely give each other short putts, take a mulligan a side, and improve their lies in a perfect fairway or a perfectly difficult patch of rough. These little things increase the enjoyment of the game, right? Actually, they allow us to delude ourselves on a regular basis. This represents a casual, friendly attack on the spirit of the game, but so what? After all, most of us don't do this for a living, as we never seem to tire of saying. And no one in particular is watching.

Really good players never do this, and this is another, perverse, way in which people justify themselves. After all, pros can afford to follow the rules to the letter. Their talent can make up for the penalty stroke on the next hole. Or they can win the tournament the week before the Masters. If the rest of us assessed ourselves all of the strokes that the rules demand, we might be ashamed to show anyone else our scorecards. It would simply be too demanding to follow all of the rules, all of the time.

The truth is that good players often miss the cut or lose tournaments because they are faithful to the rules. Sometimes, there is no reward for assessing oneself a penalty other than the understanding that one has been honest. And honesty doesn't necessarily put food on the table. There is a purity in golf, played by the rules, that is an image for human life lived at its best.

In other words, there's an honesty in golf that is good for the soul. When a player calls a penalty on himself, he may experience all sorts of feelings. Some players can quickly leave such things behind, while others may be affected by the mistake for a long time. Regardless, the score on the card is an accurate reflection of reality. Players who follow the rules present themselves to the world as they are: warts, penalties and all. There is no hiding, there is no illusion, there is no fudging. And there is no one else to blame. There's a sense of personal responsibility that can easily spill over into the rest of a player's life, if he accepts the influence of the game.

This is not to say that players who follow the rules to the letter are similarly flawless in their personal lives. The temptation to hide embarrassing or painful truths is a very strong one, as everyone knows. But they have a better than average chance to be, because of their association with the game and their playing by the rules. Every time they play, they cash in on countless opportunities to present themselves to the world as they are, to take what the game gives them (good and bad), and to take full responsibility for their actions. These are not exactly shabby qualities to take home.

But because golf is spiritual, people sometimes try to turn it into a religion. I don't have anything against religion, of course. I'd be out of a job if it didn't exist. And as long as religious practice is a corporate expression of spiritual experience, it can, and does, fulfill an important human need. The problem is that religion can become detached from its spiritual roots, and when this happens, it deteriorates into a force that does much more harm than good. Golf is susceptible to the same kind of rules fanaticism, and when it occurs, the true benefits of the game can easily be obscured.

When Craig Stadler was disqualified from a tournament because he signed an incorrect scorecard after "building a stance," his misfortune came about because at least one avid fan called the network to point out his breach of the rules. His ball had come to rest under the very low-to-the-ground branches of a pesky tree, and he had to kneel (a very religious posture, if you ask me) in order to make a pass at it. But before taking his stance, such as it was, he placed a towel on the ground, no doubt to prevent soiling the knees of his trousers. At least one viewer, however, saw something slimy in his actions. The way I see it, the viewer called because he saw golf as a religion (in its meanest manifestation) rather than as a spiritual exercise. And he justified this with the rule book.

Religion at its worst spawns all sorts of zealotry, chief among them the compulsion for rules. How else can one know who's in and who's out, who's right and who's wrong, who's been bad and who's been good? The zealot positively delights in the opportunity to point out the transgressions of others. Each breach of the rules becomes an occasion for the self-righteous to step forward and display their devotion. If enough sinners are identified and properly chastised, the zealot can call himself righteous because he remains busy enough to overlook his own transgressions, hiding them from others in the process.

Spirituality, on the other hand, begins with a number of basic assumptions, and one of the most important is the understanding that no one is blameless. While this doesn't allow people to abdicate the responsibility to speak up against what is wrong, it *does* mean that they don't use the rules as a way to get someone else. After all, who would have thought that putting a towel on the ground (with the very pristine motivation of avoiding the soiling of clothing) would constitute "building a stance"? Obviously, one person did.

The zealous approach to life is displayed by a desire to follow the law to the letter, without understanding the spirit in which it was written. Rule 13-3 states that a player "is entitled to place his feet firmly in taking his stance, but he shall not build a stance." When Stadler placed a towel on the ground, he was, in a sense, "building" a stance (even though he was on his knees). So the caller felt perfectly justified in turning him in, but he missed the point entirely.

The rule exists to remind players that they are not to do anything that would give them an unfair advantage over their opponents by manufacturing a stance more comfortable than the one the terrain gives them. The only advantage Stadler gained was to save a few bucks on his laundry bill. It was clear that he neither sought nor gained an advantage over his opponents by kneeling on a towel, because he did nothing that artificially improved his ability to hit the ball. In short, he didn't build a stance any more than he built the pyramids. By the way, had Stadler himself been a zealot, he might have pointed out that since the definition of a stance includes the word "feet," he couldn't have been building a stance while he was on his knees. Perhaps he *was* building the pyramids.

But the caller was right, at least according to the letter of the law, and the tournament officials dutifully disqualified Stadler when his signed scorecard failed to include the penalty for the violation. What else could they do? Had they ignored the caller, even on the perfectly acceptable grounds that the spirit of the law hadn't been violated, there might have been hell to pay. When zealotry is in the neighborhood, it isn't satisfied until it has a clear victim. So Stadler *had* to be offered up to satisfy whatever false god the caller worshiped.

When people turn golf into a religion, they are, at the very least, expecting more from the game than it can give. But they are also missing the spiritual benefits that the game does provide. Watching the pros apply the rules to themselves is one of them. When Hale Irwin wiffed that putt during the British Open, he immediately informed his playing companion that he had taken a four rather than a three on the hole. The truth is that the man he was paired with hadn't seen the stroke. In all likelihood, Irwin could have gotten away with it.

Yes, getting away with it was certainly an option, but he didn't even consider it. The spirit of the game demands that players be honest, that they present themselves to each other and to everyone else as they are. He could have said that he wasn't really making a pass at the ball, and his words might have been accepted. But he would still know that he actually *had* made an attempt to advance the ball. Had he put a three on his scorecard, he might have won the tournament; he'd also have found it difficult to live with himself.

This is a tremendously spiritual concept. What Irwin did was to recognize that the game is much bigger than he is, that winning isn't the sole benefit of playing the game, that it's better to live with an acknowledged mistake than it is to pretend to be blameless. And he did all of this instinctively, without hesitation. It's a testament to the spiritual qualities of the game when it's played straight up. Over time, golf has taught Irwin that the temptation to hedge a bit is always present in life, but that the urge must be resisted. To give in to the temptation is to proclaim oneself the arbiter of all truth. This is not exactly a healthy spiritual attitude. Healthy spirituality is, among other things, synonymous with rigorous honesty, not with blamelessness.

During the last round of the U.S. Open each year, the final pairing is accompanied by the top officials of the United States Golf Association and the Royal and Ancient Golf Club of St. Andrews. It's a nice tradition, but one that a zealot would be apt to misunderstand. Contrary to the opinion of those who treat golf as religion, the officials are there to interpret, rather than to enforce, the rules of the game. They *presume* that the players will enforce the rules all by themselves; for that reason, they don't bother to inspect every lie to guarantee that the players won't cheat. But they are there if the players need some assistance about how to apply a rule. And players are free to ask them for interpretations that might help them out in one situation or another. When they ask, however, it is understood that they will accept the interpretations they are given, whether favorable or not. There are, in other words, no young John McEnroes on the tour.

Golf can teach many valuable spiritual lessons. One of the most important is that the game *presumes* that competitors will play within the rules and that, when they are in doubt, they will ask for clarification. So golf begins with the understanding that people can be trusted to play the game straight up.

A touring pro or an occasional golfer who plays within the rules of the game walks an important path between two undesirable and spiritually devastating extremes. One is the temptation to delude oneself, to cheat "just a little," for whatever reason. And the other is the temptation to zealotry, the desire to use the rules as a means of breaking an opponent or of exalting oneself.

Either extreme is dangerous, because the mystery that surrounds us encompasses both justice and mercy. But we often forget one or the other. If we are being honest, we must admit that we tend to expect mercy for ourselves and the people we like and to seek justice for those who have offended us. Worse yet, we turn mercy into an excuse to let ourselves off the hook, and justice into punishment. It's difficult to embrace both. Yet golf reminds us that it's healthier to be rigorously honest about our own actions. After all, an extra stroke is not the end of the world. But there's a reason why we resist such deadly honesty.

In our society, at least, there is such an emphasis on performance that we all run the risk of becoming a little neurotic. Getting things done and doing them well are so important that we are apt to define ourselves by what we have accomplished. The temptation to compare ourselves to others in this regard is so strong that we can easily lose sight of an important spiritual value, the belief that we are loved and accepted as we are. Golf, played as it is meant to be played, presents us with a mixed bag of joy and pain, of tragedy and triumph, but it also serves to remind the attentive player that performance isn't everything, that there is something vitally important to be gained by playing it as it lies, by doing our best and accepting what comes our way. This is an immensely and spiritually healthy attitude, one that we'd all do well to adopt no matter where we are.

So I'm making an effort to abide by the rules when I play these days. But even though it's just a game, I find it hard to do. The difficulty has very little to do with golf, however. Like everyone else, I worry that what I do equals who I am. If I want to appreciate mystery, I will have to become much more honest about myself, much more willing to accept the consequences of my actions without making excuses. Golf might help me to do this, if I allow it to.

3

GETTING A GRIP

Nothing can really scare me any more, because I've seen my golf swing on tape. I had approached the viewing with relative calm, figuring that a look at my swing couldn't be all that bad and might even be encouraging. When I saw it, however, I was stunned because it did not resemble, even vaguely, the picture I had in my mind. If I had been so mistaken about the image that my swing presented to the world, my entire life could be filled with similar delusions.

I think that I had a picture of power, one that flew in the face of the results that I usually get. I envisioned smooth moving parts, each of which worked with the others to produce something that was beautiful to behold. Instead, the swing was such a confused jumble of movement that if the golf club were digitally removed from the tape, it could serve as an example of the more troubling manifestations of some nervous disorder or other. *Everything* moved, but none of the movements appeared to have a relationship to any of the others. Among other things, I began in a more or less upright position, but then I began to mimic the appearance of the tower of Pisa, first in one direction and then in the other.

I suddenly realized what everyone who had ever seen me swing a golf club knew already. I had a lousy swing. Though it was too late to destroy the evidence, that thought did cross my mind. This would have been a futile gesture, however, since people had been seeing the real thing (as opposed to the taped version) for as long as I had been playing golf. And even if I destroyed the tape as a means of sparing myself the pain of ever looking at it again, I knew that this, too, would accomplish very little. The picture was now in my memory banks and nothing short of serious therapy would shake it loose.

The difference between the tape and the picture in my head was proof that I was not the player that I liked to think I was. Before I saw the evidence, I could retain the illusion that though my swing may have looked different from that of Steve Elkington, I had the basics that the game required. I sometimes scored fairly well, and this had to mean that I could swing the club properly, didn't it? The tape said no, and the occasional good score could no longer allow me to retain the illusion.

The desire to destroy the evidence was a very human impulse, of course. All of us, at one time or another, prefer blissful ignorance to a disturbing truth. In my case, it was clear that I had preferred to believe in the beautiful picture of my swing than to suffer the inconvenience of doing what was necessary to develop one. It occurred to me that I could easily have been doing this sort of mental sleight of hand in other areas of my life, too. In other words, I now had to admit that *believing* I was a compassionate person did not actually guarantee that I *was* one. Thinking about this gave me a headache.

Secretly, I think that I always knew there was a wide gulf between reality and my perception of reality, at least on the golf course. I routinely told myself that I played reasonably well and that I had no need to seek instruction. But at times, when frustration got the better of me, I would entertain, at least temporarily, the thought that I should find a teacher. Though part of me understood that I could benefit from this, I hesitated. Seeking help was not part of my life's game plan. Cherished and long-held beliefs are difficult to root out, even when it is obvious that they are holding you back. Finally, after seeing the tape, I relented, bit the bullet, and called a teaching pro who worked with a friend of mine. But making the call and setting the appointment didn't guarantee that I'd be an eager student. Anxious, perhaps, but not exactly eager, because I feared, in a vague sort of way, that the teacher would confirm that I lacked the necessary skills.

So I devised a plan. For three days before the lesson, I spent every spare minute at the range, hitting bucket after bucket of balls. The idea, I think, was to become so good by the time the lesson came around that the pro would simply suggest minor "adjustments" in my game. In other words, I wanted to use a lesson as proof that I had no real need for instruction. I hoped that the lesson would be evidence that I had developed a game that needed only the occasional tune-up and, more important, that I had accomplished this on my own. As I pounded balls during those evening practice sessions, I had to work hard to wipe out the picture from the tape. As difficult as this was, I managed to do it. Even when I shanked or topped a ball, I dug back in and pretended that I was one swing away from the perfection that I desired, telling myself that the goal was somewhere just over the rainbow.

Of course, when I finally met with the teacher, I discovered that the days of frantic practice had only exaggerated the flaws I had developed over the years. By the time I reached the practice area that day, I didn't need fine tuning; I needed major surgery, and I was embarrassed beyond telling. My shame at not being able, on my own, to reach perfection, told me I was less comfortable with mystery than I'd like to think.

Good players have an approach to lessons that differs somewhat from mine. In the first place, they *take* them. Unlike me, they know that we can't develop and maintain a decent swing unless we have a teacher, someone who knows us and our game, someone who can notice even slight variations in a swing and can suggest remedies when it breaks down. Good players actually *welcome* lessons and the constructive criticisms that they generate. They know that they would become hopelessly lost if they insisted on going it alone, without the assistance of others. The best players even seek instruction at the first sign of trouble, thereby minimizing the chances that their games will disappear from view.

I, on the other hand, *was* hopelessly lost, with no discernible game in sight, and I had been in this fix since I had first picked up a club. Worse than that, I didn't *know* that I was lost, even though the results of my swing often contained incontrovertible evidence that this was so. As I said, I had deluded myself into thinking that my swing was fine, and I didn't want anything out of the ordinary (like the truth) to get in the way of the image that I carried around in my head. Though I needed instruction, I preferred to pretend that I did not. And when reality finally crashed through all of my illusions and it became obvious that I needed help, I was embarrassed, as if the need for instruction made me somehow defective.

I know now that recognizing the need for instruction is perhaps the first step toward improving your game. In other words, no one becomes Jack Nicklaus simply by being born. Golf is far too complicated a game to master. Better players realize that, to a great degree, progress is directly proportional to the desire to seek out and to accept the best help available. This is known as enlightenment.

The rest of us, even if we submit to an occasional lesson, prefer to live with the illusion that we are just one bucket of balls away from becoming the players we have always dreamed of being. Even players less talented than we are could look at our swings and make helpful suggestions, but we are not interested in soliciting (or accepting) any advice. We are sure that we can do it by ourselves. In fact, we believe that we *need* to do it ourselves. That way, we can avoid sharing any of the credit for our triumphs. While we might consider this a clever way to prove ourselves, we actually eliminate many opportunities for success when we adopt this attitude.

Perhaps we assume this rugged individualist pose because we see so many different types of swings when we watch a tournament on television. Some swings are so wildly unorthodox that trying to emulate them might result in complicated orthopedic surgery. Raymond Floyd and Kenny Perry are good examples. Despite the awkward appearance of their swings, these players (and many others) manage to get the job done. Of course, I take these unusual but successful swings as further proof that it's solely up to me to develop a swing that will lower my scores.

Yet these less than picture-perfect swings are surely the result of wise instruction. It's simply that the people who taught these players didn't make them conform to some kind of ideal swing. As long as they managed to deliver the clubhead to the ball in an efficient and repeatable way, they were allowed to develop a swing that felt natural to them. So these players benefited from having teachers who knew them and their talents and who helped them to apply their gifts in ways that enabled them to reach their potential.

All of this indicates that good instruction tends to accentuate our natural gifts. There are, in other words, many ways to skin a cat. Without instruction, however, we tend to develop a swing that approximates an attempt literally to skin a rather large and understandably less than cooperative cat. And all the while, we think that our swings are as fluid as that of Sam Snead.

Golf can teach many spiritual lessons, and among the most important is the reminder that human beings are capable of deceiving themselves. We can mistake black for white with ease. Seeing myself on tape destroyed (for a time) any illusions I had about my swing, but it wasn't long before I desired a return to self-diagnosis. After briefly entertaining the notion that a little help couldn't hurt, I returned to my usual modus operandi, believing that I was the only teacher I ever needed. This is evidence that believing we need no help is one of the most destructive delusions of all.

We might be better off if we *began* each day with the presumption that there was a gap between reality and how we perceive it. If we did, we might be more willing to seek some honest input. In golf, as in other areas of life, it never hurts to take a lesson, since it's one of the better ways to discover the truth about ourselves and to minimize our faults. Shying away from a little help is a sure sign that we prefer delusion to an honest appraisal of ourselves. It's also a remarkably clever way to place obstacles along the path to fulfillment. An example of a different kind demonstrates what I mean.

I don't dance very well. In fact, I don't dance much at all, solely because of my aversion to asking for the help that I need. As I was becoming a teenager, it became clear to me that I would, at some time, be expected to dance with someone before I moved on to college. This created a problem for me. In a curious reversal of my belief about my golf swing, I *knew* that I would appear awkward if I stepped onto a dance floor. I needed no evidence; I was sure that I would invite ridicule if I tried even a few steps.

I had very little excuse not to learn, because a more than willing teacher was living in my house. My younger sister, who has never shunned a challenge in her life, was a good dancer, and she was determined to show me how. As it turned out, however, her desire to help me was no match for my stubborn refusal to accept anything other than my version of the truth. And the truth, according to me, was that I couldn't do it. As a result, I navigated my way through adolescence by steering clear of danger (and of my sister as well), only occasionally getting my feet wet with a slow dance or two. I missed out on a lot of fun because I wouldn't subject my version of the truth to a little scrutiny.

We all do this sort of thing from time to time. When I was in high school, I also refused to put any effort into math because I didn't like it. At the time, I thought that I was fortunate to have friends who were very good at math and who allowed me, on occasion, to copy their work. I told myself that I engaged in this little conspiracy because I wasn't good at algebra or trigonometry. But the truth was that, just like dancing, I never gave the subjects a chance. As long as I could slide by, I took advantage of my friends' "help" and justified myself quite easily. This didn't help much when tests came around, of course, but that didn't matter to me back then. One way or another, I could usually figure out just enough to pass, and that was all I was looking for anyway.

I felt the occasional stab of guilt, as you can imagine. After all, I was cheating, and this was clearly wrong. I knew, to some extent, that I was deluding myself when I found ways to justify my behavior, but what I failed to realize was even worse. Only later did I come to see that I actually could learn the math, that I had a talent for it far beyond what I credited myself with. It would have taken some work, and some help from teachers and friends, but I could have done pretty well with a little effort. Instead, I danced around the problem (the only kind of dancing I truly appreciate), getting by when I could actually have achieved some success. I never came even remotely close to seeing this at the time. Since I *knew* I couldn't do it, I also *knew* it would be futile to try.

I thought the only problem was that I was cheating, and though this was certainly true, the greater problem was that I failed to see my potential because I believed that if math did not come naturally, without a lot of exertion, I couldn't really do it. I had deluded myself into thinking that I was only good at things that entailed very little effort on my part. In other words, if I needed instruction to unlock my potential, I decided that I didn't *have* any potential. This became my excuse for cheating, a true enemy of the spiritual life. But the greater enemy remained my aversion to help, which everyone needs.

I displayed this same resistance to instruction in golf, as I have already mentioned. But the game presented me with an opportunity to change, as math and dancing never could have. The difference, of course, was that I *liked* golf and that I desperately wanted to become good at it. When I first took up the game, my parents suggested that I spend an afternoon with a friend of the family who happened to be the pro at a club not far from the town where we lived. He was a patient and gentle man, and he agreed to help me out. Because I had the desire to play well, I grudgingly accepted a lesson.

He was a good teacher, too, especially because he was left-handed, and because he used this as a teaching tool. He suggested that we line up across from each other so that I could use him as a mirror. If I followed his lead and brought the club back and through as he did, I could actually "see" what my swing ought to look like, as I felt it in myself. It seemed like a good idea, and I was enthused about it for a while, especially when his instruction produced some good results. But then the same thoughts that have always been just below the surface came into play. After he had shown me some things and I had managed to include them, temporarily, in my swing, I decided that I didn't need him anymore. I could take what he had given me and become whatever I wanted to be.

Years later, when I saw on tape the swing that I had developed, I thought about him. What I had produced looked nothing like the mirror he had held up to me when I was a kid. I had been certain that I needed no help, that I could do it all by myself. Because of that attitude, I had strayed so far that I wondered if I could find my way back, even with the help of an entire squad of professionals.

The truth is that no one can do it alone, that we very

much need people to provide mirrors for us. The problem is that we are often unwilling to look into the mirrors that they hold up to us. Back when I was allowed to copy my friends' homework, I was sure that I had it made. In truth, I needed someone to help me actually learn the subject. Occasionally one of them tried, but I refused to look into that mirror, preferring instead to find someone else who would be willing to let me have his homework. Each time that I found a willing co-conspirator, I allowed my aversion to instruction to convince me that this was the only way out, that I didn't have what it took to do math. Nothing could have been further from the truth, but I wasn't interested in the truth just then.

People hold mirrors up to us all the time, or at least they try to. But the human tendency is either to refuse to look closely or to see what we wish to see in spite of the evidence. I could have known how much I needed golf lessons if I had paid even minimal attention to the shots I usually hit (or to the small offers of advice from my playing companions), but I preferred to believe that I had the loveliest of swings rather than to ask for anyone else's opinion. It's no surprise that I would choose to live this way on the golf course. I had, after all, been behaving the same way in other areas of my life for as long as I could remember.

Whenever I said something that hurt a friend, for example, the look on her face was all the mirror I needed, but I usually chose to believe that I was compassionate enough and that she simply needed to start living in the real world. If I held a grudge when someone hurt me, I acted as if this were a perfectly natural response and that my view of the world was the only one that counted, even when I was aware, deep down, that I tended to wear my feelings on my sleeve. I was so used to deluding myself and sanctifying my own attitudes about myself and other people that it's no surprise I spent all of those years creating a terrible golf swing and telling myself that it was the picture of perfection.

The saddest part of this is that golf had always presented me with opportunities to face my delusions and to do something about ridding myself of some of them, both on and off the course. But I chose to believe in the picture in my mind rather than the reality that everyone could see. When I finally decided to take that lesson, things had gotten out of hand, as I have already said. And I was suffering from a lot more delusions than I'd care to talk about.

One of the reasons that I was such a pro at avoiding lessons was that I *pretended* to take them on occasion. If my game were going south, I might ask a friend for a little advice. At times like these, however, I was merely looking for a temporary band-aid, a hint that could carry me through until I could bring my game around on my own. I managed to avoid wondering when this would happen. In similar fashion, I occasionally asked a friend to tell me what he thought about me, whether or not, for example, I had handled a certain situation well. But I always chose wisely, meaning that I always asked someone who was likely to tell me what I wanted to hear. If the friend told me anything else, I'd thank him and promptly forget what he had said.

This is why it was such a radical step to call a pro. I knew, somewhere inside of me, that it was going to be a painful experience, despite all of the frantic practice I had engaged in beforehand. I called, even though I was aware that I was inviting a situation which might force me to give up some of my illusions about myself. I only made the appointment because golf (or at least the way I was playing golf) had become intolerable. I figured that a lesson couldn't be worse than playing had become. It's the old axiom that people in the recovery movement refer to all of the time. When a person experiences enough pain, he'll ask for the help he has needed all along. This does not mean, however, that he will like the idea or that he will immediately change his ways.

I admitted that I needed the help of a professional, because even submitting to instruction was preferable to one more day of frustration on the course. Yet I retained some hope that it would all prove unnecessary, that I still needed only the band-aid that I usually looked for. So after I had spent the evenings before the lesson hitting countless balls, I drove to the appointed place. When I met the teacher at the practice range, he did something that I have never forgotten. He asked to shake hands, so I took his hand and squeezed it with my usual end-of-the-world grip. I had always supposed that firmness in a handshake was measured in pounds of pressure per square inch, and my teacher winced as we stood there in the afternoon sunlight.

I could tell that he was impressed, and I expected him to say something like, "Well, you certainly have a manly hand-shake there." Instead, he started by saying that if I used the same stranglehold on a golf club that I had applied to his hand, my grip pressure was the first thing I needed to change. He had no idea what he was getting into.

The lesson was clearly getting off on the wrong foot. If this was an example of his golf philosophy, we were sure to have problems. All of my life, I had figured that good results were a product of strenuous effort. In other words, the harder I tried, the more I would succeed. It followed that strangling the golf club was the first step in the process of bringing the game to its knees.

On the other hand, even a milligram of honesty would have forced me to admit that I had been the one on my knees most of the time. But delusion is a powerful thing. The way I preferred to see it, my teacher simply needed to give me the few tips I needed to round out my game. These would be little insider secrets that can only be passed down by gurus who have, in turn, been taught the secrets by older masters. I was willing to accept nothing more than this, because then I wouldn't be my own savior.

Instead, I learned that my entire approach to the game was misguided, at best. This very fine teacher made it clear to me that I needed an entire reorientation to the game. But as he tried to help me build a game from the ground up, he began to understand how difficult this would be. I had spent my entire life preparing myself to resist anything of value he might teach me.

When he showed me a better way to grip the club, he spent very little time with the position of my hands, insisting instead that my grip pressure had to decrease by a factor of ten or so. But if I tried to hold the club that loosely, I was certain that it would fly out of my hand. I also just *knew* that a person could never hit a golf ball very far unless he were holding the club in a death grip. I was following my usual pattern. I was not about to allow someone who was better at golf than I was tell me how to play the game. It turned out, however, that he could be as persistent as I was.

For the longest time, he had me set up to the ball and take the club back about half way. Each time that I addressed the ball, he'd remind me to relax my hands. And each time, I'd relax them a little bit. But as I started to bring the club back, my grip would tighten, and he'd look at me as if there was some language problem between us. In a way, there was.

I *understood* the words he was using, of course, but I didn't *believe* that following his advice could possibly result in the kind of swing that would bring me any success. The problem was that his instruction ran counter to my entire approach to life. Whenever I had encountered a difficult problem, especially when I didn't achieve the level of success that I desired, I always redoubled my efforts. On rare occasions, this had worked for me, so I had naturally adopted this method as my basic approach to everything, except when I began by believing that I couldn't do something (like math). So when I took up golf and discovered that it was a difficult game, I was faced with two basic choices. I could give up, or I could try harder. I don't like to think of myself as a quitter (I always conveniently forget about algebra), so only one option was really open to me.

Of course, trying harder meant increasing the intensity of my attack. So as time went on, I gripped the club harder and swung with more force. Because the added pressure and speed increased by gradual increments, I hardly noticed them at all. By the time I went for the lesson that day, I swung at the speed of light, and I held the club as if it were the throat of a dangerous enemy. It's no wonder that I had developed a swing that even a mother couldn't love.

I was spiritually unprepared for that lesson because I didn't appreciate the value of lessons in the first place. My teacher's words might as well have been spoken in another language. It turned out that virtually everything I did at golf was done with about ten times as much force as was necessary to hit the ball successfully. By my way of looking at things, this meant that I should have been ten times better than anyone else, but this was obviously not the case.

My teacher explained to me (very patiently, under the circumstances) that the clubhead would gather much greater speed if I paid more attention to relaxing my grip pressure. This didn't compute very well. Even when I managed, after a few false starts, to hit some shots with a more relaxed grip and found that I liked the results, I still didn't want to believe what I was seeing. It didn't feel as if I were trying at all. Nothing I cared about in life was supposed to be this easy. A bit of irony was trying to force its way into my consciousness. All those times when I had hit poor shots in the past, I kept replaying the tape of the beautiful swing I had in my head. But when I was on the range with my teacher, hitting some really nice shots, I couldn't begin to picture the smooth movements that had brought those shots about.

Could it be that my teacher was trying to tell me that golf was going to be about as difficult as I decided to make it? Was he subtly trying to tell me that to refuse instruction was to guarantee that whatever I tried was bound to be more difficult than it had to be? Was he attempting to close the gap between what I thought my swing looked like and what it actually was?

As I stood on the practice range with my teacher that day, I realized that, in addition to the help with my game, he was presenting me with an entirely new way of thinking about life in general, and about the spiritual journey in particular. If I could adjust my opinion about what golf lessons could do for me and accept similar instruction in other areas of my life, I might do more than lower my score.

We are, of course, responsible for ourselves, but all too often, this perception of responsibility leads us to draw false conclusions. Among the deadliest of these is the belief that everything depends upon us. In other words, we become willing prisoners of an overdeveloped sense of responsibility. When this is our starting point, we have only two options. We can either give up and abdicate all responsibility, or we can jump in feet first and try to overpower everything that comes our way.

On the golf course, this leads to the creation of a swing like mine. Composed entirely of physical effort and fraught with tension even before address, such a swing is long on determination but short on the rhythm and tempo necessary to get the job done. Each new failure cries out for even greater efforts, and repeated failures can convince a person to give up the game entirely. Walking away from the game, however, is an admission that one doesn't have what it takes. This is why I have quit golf hundreds of times. It is also the reason I have come back to it, convinced of my need to figure it out on my own.

All people who play golf are tempted, at least from time to time, to rush to one extreme or the other. But we fail to see that there is an alternative which steers between the extremes of giving up and digging even deeper holes for oneself. The alternative is to seek instruction. While this requires that we admit the possibility that our picture of ourselves is inaccurate, it also provides an opportunity for each of us to create an entirely new set of pictures that bring perception and reality closer to unity.

One of the more important elements of the spiritual journey is the willingness to see ourselves as others see us, rather than to maintain the willful thought that we are who we wish to be simply because we wish it. It never hurts to ask others what they see in us, but we succumb far too often to the temptation to leave well enough alone, even when we know, deep down, that well enough isn't close to where we desire to be.

This truth has tried to present itself to me on many occasions, but seeing my swing on tape was one of the clearest examples I have ever experienced. The reality of who I am is often way out of synch with the image which I insist on seeing. I suffer from a number of serious delusions about myself, about what gifts I have, and about how well or how poorly I am using them. Despite a sometimes overwhelming volume of evidence to the contrary, I often prefer to believe that the world would be better off conforming to me; I don't like to entertain the notion that I have to change anything about myself, even when my experience tells me that something is terribly wrong. I am, in short, a human being.

One of the mysteries we encounter is the mystery of ourselves. The truth about who we are is often buried beneath a confused jumble of postures and poses, of delusion and denial. But we slowly make sense of the mystery through relationships. We learn more about ourselves each time we ask for the honest appraisal of people who know us. We must invite that appraisal, however, and be willing to accept it at face value if it is to be of any use to us.

My almost lifelong association with golf has provided me with endless opportunities to see that there is often a wide gap between the person I wish to be and the person I really am. It has also provided me with examples of people who routinely seek out the help they need to close that gap in themselves. When I think of Jack Nicklaus working with a teacher after all that he has accomplished, I am reminded of a great spiritual truth: no one can ever afford to say, or even to think, that he or she has arrived. To do so is to risk widening the gulf between reality and one's perception of it. Whether we are trying to improve our game or to become more compassionate or forgiving, we need to be willing, perhaps eager, to ask for the help we need.

Golf, like life, is difficult to do well, and it is impossible to do well unaided. And the game is a particularly helpful teacher because the lessons are not nearly as painful on the practice range as they are in other areas of life. Face it; it's much easier to admit that my short game is a wreck than to entertain the possibility that I am thoughtless or judgmental. But if I ask someone to help me with my chipping or putting and the result is that I improve, I become less reluctant to paper over my personal shortcomings and to accept the help I need to change. The rewards can be startling. For example, seeking help might allow me to avoid ever seeing anything resembling my horrible golf swing reflected in the eyes of someone I care about.

4

TAKING IT BACK

On any number of occasions, an afternoon at the golf course has become a painful experience, one that I wouldn't wish upon anybody. The round usually begins tamely enough, but as it progresses, everything deteriorates and I find that I have dug myself a hole that threatens to bury me. By the time I have reached this point, my thoughts and feelings have become so extreme that I cannot trust even the simplest idea or emotion. But these extremes of thinking and feeling (which I talked about in chapter one) are, during some rounds, merely the symptoms which I recognize at the surface. A greater problem lies much deeper within me.

I had another dreadful experience recently, and as I think about it now, I believe that I am on the threshold of an important insight. It has eluded me in the past, but the most recent terror was so intense that I cannot shake it. It clings to me like a soggy sweatshirt that can only be peeled, with difficulty, from my sagging body. So rather than struggling to get the shirt off, I have decided to let it stay on for a while. Perhaps in golf, as in the spiritual quest, moments of despair can become opportunities for growth, for new life and new possibilities. If we allow the bad times to linger (rather than to seek ways to make them disappear), we might just discover what they can tell us about ourselves.

If anyone had ever asked, I'd have told them that I have a passion for golf. I suppose that those who know me well fall into two categories: those who pity me and those who think that I'm lucky to have such a nice diversion. In fact, I've often told people, even when they have not asked, that I find golf perfectly relaxing. When I'm playing, I tell them, I think of nothing else at all. The implication is that golf allows me to get away from all of the demands of my life, that it helps me put things into perspective. This is not exactly true, however, because golf (at least the way I play golf) often tends to confirm my worst beliefs about myself, rather than lead me to new and helpful insights.

I may not think about my job when I'm on the course, but what I *am* thinking about makes me anything but relaxed. Yet this little truth had always escaped me, until I played the round I have so far only alluded to. While I may insist that I'm out to have a good time when I'm on the course, I actually eliminate many opportunities to enjoy myself because I am constantly haunted by the past and worried as hell about the future.

As I began the round in question, I stood on the first tee, consumed by the same feeling I have experienced hundreds of times before. My partner was a friend who is a good player, and I remembered how poorly I had played the last time we had been out together. This round, I told myself, would be different. By the time it was my turn to tee it up, I was already making promises to myself about what my score would be at the turn. Of course, I would have to play a lot better than I usually do to post that kind of score. At first, these "positive" thoughts seemed a good idea, a way to motivate myself to concentrate and thus to play better, but they soon transformed themselves into a cold, hard knot in my stomach.

And the feeling didn't exactly diminish when my drive came to rest forty yards or so short of my playing companion's ball. By the time we reached the sixth hole, my game was in a shambles, but the decline had begun as I stood over the approach shot in the first fairway. We had each hit one shot, and I was already behind in my quest to equal his performance. I knew that I would have to ratchet my game up several notches if I were to give him any sort of match at all. This is not what any reasonable person would call relaxation.

Everything about the round was extreme. When I managed to hit a fairly good shot, I experienced a moment of elation. It was coming around, I told myself. But as I stood over the approach shot and concentrated on duplicating the swing, I became as tense and twitchy as a squirrel. The next shot then dribbled about fifty yards down the fairway. Frustration set in, and I was soon telling myself that I'd never learn how to play this game. On one hole, I found myself wondering how much I could get if I sold all of my clubs, balls and assorted paraphernalia; on the next, I was consulting my calendar to see when I could squeeze in some time at the range. These mutually exclusive thoughts seemed reasonable to me and arrived with the same intensity. In the midst of these musings, I began to sense that there was something seriously wrong with my approach to the game.

Jack Nicklaus arrived at the twelfth tee at Augusta during one round of the 1995 Masters and promptly shanked the ball. The crowd around the tee numbered in the hundreds, if not the thousands, and the television audience was probably in the millions. When he hit the shot and the camera zoomed in on him, he looked a little sheepish. Who could blame him? The ever-present microphones picked up his words as he told the crowd that he'd hit a similar shot from this tee once before (the 1964 Masters, if I'm not mistaken). Then he walked to his ball and made a decent recovery from a difficult spot.

How I felt for him after he hit that shot! And I'm sure that I was much more nervous than he was as he stood over the next one. Had I been in his place, that one muffed shot would almost certainly have guaranteed another. I'd have been so upset at making such a mistake that the presence of the crowd would have caused me to go into convulsions in anticipation of the next chance to make a spectacle of myself.

I am beginning to understand that this is one of the keys to my poor play. There are obviously many differences between me and Jack Nicklaus, but one of them is very clear. When Nicklaus stands over the ball, it is simply another golf shot. When I am preparing to hit a shot, *everything* is on the line. Because this is the case, he can play and then forget a poor shot, while my many poor shots encircle me like so many witnesses for the prosecution. And I am always guilty as charged.

The witnesses line up to accuse me because I live in the past and in the future on the golf course, just as I tend to do in other areas of my life. I suffer when I fall short of perfection, and this leads me to worry that the future will be as poor as the past has proved itself to be. It's a sort of black and white approach to living that I have elevated to an art form, and it brings me nothing but misery. Right or wrong, good or bad, on or off.

This hit me as never before when I thought about the round I played with that friend. One of the major differences between me and good players is that they can get over a bad shot because it never threatens to define them. But one of my deepest fears is that *all* of my shots define me. One moment I'm good, the next I'm bad, and on balance I'm pretty far below average. Not that I lead a very balanced life, of course. I spend a good bit of my time, on the course and off, rushing back and forth from a past which will not go away and the future which is arriving way too fast.

I'm sure that some very fine players engage in worry about the past and future as I do. But they are good players in part because they have seized some of the opportunities to learn the valuable lessons which golf provides. Life is difficult, as everyone knows, and no one really masters it. To expect perfection is to pave the way for disappointment. To allow mistakes to define us is to make life far more painful and difficult than it has to be, and to be consumed with the past is to set ourselves up to create a miserable future because so much is on the line. It's true that most people *know* these things, but few people act as if they actually *believe* them.

So I don't so much have a passion for golf as I have a desire, maybe even a need, to become perfect. But I can't become flawless unless I can somehow change the past and guarantee the future. It's ironic that I've chosen the most difficult of games and then applied my desire for perfection to it, but the greater irony is that although golf has always presented me with opportunities to question some of my basic assumptions, I have managed to squander them all until now. In essence, I have been so intent on becoming perfect that I have failed to appreciate that it cannot be done.

I can't change the past, and the future hasn't happened yet. Though these truths are self-evident, I live as if I could rewrite the laws of nature. When I employ the present as a means of overcoming the past and of securing a mistake-free future, the present becomes intolerable because neither desire is possible. In fact, I come pretty close to guaranteeing a future that's a copy of the past when I am trying to make up for the past in the first place. As a result, I make myself perfectly miserable because I fall short of the perfection that I desire.

These are tough lessons, and they are very difficult to learn in the midst of the daily grind of life, especially because other people sometimes seem to be demanding that we solve both the past and the future for them. But in the relative tranquillity of the golf course, perhaps we can see how such expectations harm us, regardless of their origin. Because the stakes are not as high when we are playing golf, we can afford to tinker with things a bit, to try on new approaches, and to see how they fit.

Every day, we encounter people who appear to be just fine, but who suffer in ways we are unaware of. Sometimes, we are those people. The pain occasionally takes the form of a past that we cannot escape or a future that scares the hell out of us. Often, it's both at the same time, because worry about the future often springs from guilt about the past. No one is immune from this sort of pain. The only recourse at times is to insist (at least secretly) that we experience worry about the past and the future because we care. Only insensitive jerks can forget the past or wait for the future to arrive on its own. Maybe this is why Fred Couples takes a lot a flak from people who don't know better.

During the early stages of Sunday's coverage of the 1995 Masters, CBS was scrambling to present all of the action live. It was a hopeless enterprise, because it seemed that many important events were happening simultaneously. Just as one player was chipping to the tenth green, someone else was putting for birdie on number sixteen. There were a lot of stories out there, and they were all unfolding, as they say, at once.

In the midst of this frantic enterprise, the cameras switched to number eight, just in time to see the aftermath of Fred Couples' swing. It was his second shot to the par five, and as every lover of Augusta National knows, it's blind. Since the cut to his swing had come late, and since something else was happening on another hole, the director ordered another camera into action. Viewers merely saw Couples walk casually toward his caddie to hand him the club.

As the camera caught the next important moment, TV viewers could hear a roar from somewhere else on the course. A few minutes later, a replay informed them that Couples' approach had been nearly perfect. The ball had followed the contour of the green and then come to rest two inches or so from the cup. A certain eagle, and almost a

double eagle, because the ball had slipped by the edge of the
cup before coming to rest. It was a spectacular result that
stood in stark contrast to Couples' initial casual reaction.

This is exactly the sort of thing that drives some golf
enthusiasts wild. When I saw Couples after he hit the shot,
I presumed that he had hit a poor one, because of the way
that he let the club go with one hand and sauntered away. I
suppose that few, if any, of the viewers had a clue that his
shot was as good as it actually was.

Couples is always doing this. Oh, I know that he occasionally says something encouraging to the golf ball as it
approaches its target. Usually, he says, "Get down," to a particularly long drive, and I recall that he said, "Go," to his
approach at eighteen in the final round of a tournament that
he won toward the end of 1994. But that's about as animat-
ed as he gets, and he's quite a contrast to a lot of other players on the tour in this regard.

Many of the pros use all sorts of body English in their
attempts to make the ball do something that they want it to
do. Some berate themselves loudly whenever they hit a poor
shot. Regardless, we can usually tell by their demeanor what
kind of shot they've hit. If nothing else, the cameras catch a
telltale facial expression that informs us whether the ball is
headed toward a trap or the pin.

But Couples gives very few clues, and a lot of people fault
him for this. They see his lack of animation as an indication
that he doesn't care. Using this as their measure, they say
that he'd win everything in sight if he had a little fire in his
belly. And because he doesn't win every time he goes out,
they accuse him of being a slacker. Unreasonable expectations aside, it seems to me that people who think in this way
miss the point.

I like to think that what other people call Fred's lack of
motivation is actually an indication of an extraordinary spiritual gift. More than any other player out there, Couples is
aware that once the ball has left the clubface, it is quite lit-

erally out of his hands. What's done is done, and no amount of coaxing, crying, commanding, or cajoling will have any effect on a ball in flight. Perhaps the wind will catch an errant shot and help it out a bit, but it's just as likely to make a poor shot come out worse. In any event, the die has been cast, as Julius Caesar used to say. As I recall, people used to find fault with *him*, too.

Most amateurs are the exact opposite of Couples. They go into all sorts of contortions on the course, and though experience has taught them that none of their gyrations or verbal exhortations has ever had a positive effect on a shot, they continue to search for some new move that will bring them success. The truth is that the results are often out of their hands *before* they hit a shot, either because they are thinking about the last poor shot as they stand over the ball or because they are counting on this shot to somehow erase a lifetime of poor ball striking.

What I'm trying to say is that Fred Couples' attitude after he has hit a shot is healthy, from a spiritual point of view. There is truly no point in worrying about a shot after you have hit it. That time has passed, and it's not yet time to worry about the next shot. If Fred Couples has taken what he has learned about golf shots and applied it to the rest of his life, then he is more spiritually advanced than a lot of people I know.

This is yet another indication that the lessons golf teaches can help a person along the path to spiritual growth. One of the most important lessons, in life and in golf, is that all we can do at any moment is the best we can do. No amount of worrying about or reliving the past will change it in the slightest. In this regard, Couples presents the image of spiritual advancement. He sometimes slips up and tries to alter the ball in flight, but, as I've already said, nobody is perfect. Regardless, no one seems to let go of the past as quickly or completely as he does.

When people fault Fred Couples for what appears to be

his lack of concern on the golf course, they are, in all likelihood, demonstrating the very attitude that holds them back. We care so much, we try so hard, that we work against ourselves. Our games suffer because we want it all, and we want it *now*. And one poor shot begets another because we cannot let it go.

Perhaps we do this because our lives are filled with a similar desire to have no regrets about the past. Maybe we care so much about everything because each moment of our lives is do or die, life or death, all or nothing. Perhaps we spend a lot of time living in the past, hoping that if we relive a mistake enough times, we will find a way to change it. Maybe we are so concerned about securing a mistake-free future that we make it impossible to perform well in the present or even simply to enjoy what we are doing.

If that's our attitude, we could probably learn a lot from watching Fred Couples on the weekends. We could all certainly do a lot worse than to adopt his attitude toward our golf shots and the rest of our lives. The idea is to do the best we can and to learn from our mistakes. Once it's left the clubhead—or our mouths—it's gone forever. Good or bad, we'd be better off if we could let it go and move on.

When we allow ourselves to be consumed by the past and to work desperately to relive it or somehow to make up for it, we are actually allowing the past to define us. In doing so, we are increasing the odds that the past will recreate itself precisely because it matters so much to us.

Letting go of the past is difficult, God knows. But it is an essential component of spiritual progress, as is the ability to plan for the future without letting it scare us to death. This is why watching good players can help us to tune up our spiritual engines.

Good players know (and poorer players would benefit from knowing) that to worry about the past or the future is to waste time and energy. And it's not just because the past is gone and the future isn't here yet. It's that when we are in the past or the future, we cannot bring our skills to focus on the present. In other words, the present becomes impossible and intolerable when we are living in either the past or the future.

One of the most important attributes that good players possess is the knowledge that they can't play all eighteen holes at once. This is another one of those self-evident truths that many of us manage to forget. In fact, a person can really play only one shot at a time. While the pros may be thinking ahead to the kind of approach they'd like to have on a particular hole, they don't get so consumed by it that they cannot adjust if the tee shot winds up in another place. And once a hole is gone, there is literally no point in thinking about it again (at least until the round is complete). Going back over a completed round is a good idea, as long as the purpose is to learn from one's mistakes. Healthy use of the past is one of the methods by which good players get that way, just as healthy regard for the immediate future enables them to act wisely in the present.

Good spiritual health depends upon a recognition of the possible and the impossible. For example, while it's obvious that we can't live our entire life in one moment, this doesn't prevent us from trying to do it. Sometimes we trick ourselves into saying that we are concerned with the past because we wish to learn from it, just like good players or wise people. While this is the only thing the past is good for, we often flagellate ourselves with the past rather than deal with it and then leave it behind. And while wise people do plan for the future, we often must admit, if we're being honest, that we look to the future in attempts to control it before it arrives.

This living in the past and the future creates a lot of unnecessary pain. How many of us spend the rest of our lives regretting some past mistake, even though God and everyone else have forgotten about it long ago? And how often do we worry ourselves sick about a future that never comes to pass, and which all of our concern wouldn't have prevented anyway?

Golf is spiritual because it *demands* that a player remain in the present, at least if she or he wants to achieve any success at all. It turns out that a life well lived demands this same focus on the moment. No matter what we are doing, the present is a middle path which steers between the extremes of the past and the future. All of us tend to veer off toward one or another of the extremes, and some of us are good at moving toward the past and the future simultaneously. If we thought about it at all, we would realize that a preoccupation with either the past or the future robs us of the energy that we need in the present. Golf can help us to see this, because the rewards or punishments for straying from the present are so clear and so immediate. Thus it is far easier to see how remaining in the present can help us. In addition, the stakes are relatively low on the golf course, but we might decide to take what we've learned into our other endeavors.

I will never have Fred Couples' game, but I'm trying to adopt the attitude he seems to have when he's playing. He presents an image of one of the most important elements of the spiritual journey: the ability to stay in the present, without being haunted by the past or consumed by the future. So I no longer shout commands to a ball in flight, and I don't hit my next shot until I have forgotten the last one, good or bad. I'm convinced that the more I do this, the better will be my chances to live without being consumed by regrets or by unnecessary worry about the future. The present is mysterious enough all by itself.

If you look at it from a certain angle, you can see that golf is a gift from God, for whom there is no past or future, just an eternally manageable present. It's a good place to live.

5

THE LONG
AND SHORT OF IT

I was raised to be modest, but I believe in honesty, too; so I am forced to admit that I used to be a pretty good player on the practice tee. But then I should have been, because I spent an inordinate amount of time there. Like a lot of high handicappers, I found it difficult to resist the temptation to grab a few bags of balls and swing away at them. This provided me with hours of mindless exercise, but it didn't even come close to making me a better player, as honesty also demands that I admit.

As long as I'm being so forthright, I should also say that my occasional successes on the range occurred only under very specific circumstances. It sometimes happened that my first few swings were good enough to produce relatively nice shots, but this was only because I was not sufficiently warmed up to swing as hard as I really liked to. But even if a few easy swings resulted in good shots, I eventually started *really* swinging, and the same thing happened every time. The harder I swung, the worse I hit the ball.

I compounded this by engaging in other, terrible habits. When I hit a really bad shot, I immediately teed another one up. Part of me realized that a practice swing might not hurt, or that doing my preshot routine (such as it was) would have been a good idea. But I didn't believe that I had time for this, because I wanted to get the bad shot out of my mind as quickly as possible, and I figured that another shot was the only way to do it. This hurry-up attitude often produced another poor shot, and the sequence repeated itself until I began to wear myself out.

Then I became a good player again. By the time I had hit a hundred balls or so, most of them with maximum effort, my swing slowed down through attrition. I simply had too little energy left to bring my usual monster swing into play. Lo and behold, I began hitting fairly good shots again, especially when I was too tired to bring the club all the way back to my left ankle, as I am wont to do. So toward the end of my time on the practice range, the percentage of good shots increased.

On principle, I never left the range on a bad shot. Even if I was ready for the paramedics, I stayed there, hitting shot after shot, until I hit one that satisfied me (even if I had to liberate range balls from other people when they were not looking). Despite the fatigue that my routine caused, I was never too tired to pose after I managed somehow to hit a shot I was proud of. It was sometimes difficult to see if anyone was looking, but I have fairly good peripheral vision. Just in case someone had been looking without my noticing, I learned to reach for another ball in a casual manner that told anyone who happened to be watching that this sort of thing went on all of the time. Ho hum, another perfect five iron.

I know that plenty of people might cringe as they read this, because they are out there on the range, pounding balls without purpose day after day, just as I used to do. And because they do this without the benefit of a teacher, they simply reinforce all the bad habits that they have developed over the years. If they get into a groove, it's by accident, which only compounds the frustration, because they have no idea at all how to recreate what they've stumbled upon. The range becomes a place to lose a little weight, but never a place to learn anything of value.

Oftentimes, as I walked to or crawled back from the range, I saw other players practicing the short game, on or around the practice green, putting or chipping. Perhaps they were in the practice bunker, trying a variety of shots from troublesome lies. I even witnessed people throwing balls into the high grass around the practice area, presenting themselves with horrible shots to recover from. As I passed them on the way to the range, I told myself that I'd probably benefit from a similar routine or even that I'd practice those shots later. But by the time I'd hit all of those full shots at the range, I was far too tired to do anything but head for the nineteenth hole.

Those days, it almost never occurred to me that a three foot putt counts exactly the same as a drive of three hundred yards. It never dawned on me that I could improve my score much more quickly if I devoted some time to the short game. In fact, if I had devoted half the time to my short game that I spent on full shots, I'd probably have lowered my score appreciably (and permanently), because I actually putt fairly well without practicing at all. But hitting putts and chips was far less satisfying than swinging away; I got a greater thrill from hitting a good, full five iron than I did from holing a putt, even a long one. This, alone, might have told me something.

Because I didn't practice this part of the game much at all, I made lots of poor little shots that otherwise might have turned out better, had I spent some time working on them. And since my full shots were erratic as well (because of the routine I followed on the practice tee), I didn't improve much at all. Then I wondered why I couldn't lower my handicap.

Back then, it was a misnomer even to refer to my shots around the green as a short game, because I really had no short game at all. Instead, I brought the same mindless, all-or-nothing approach to the short shots that I applied to all of those full shots at the range. In short, I had never met a delicate chip or pitch that I didn't think I could bull my way through, as if sheer force were all that the game required. This attitude produced two extreme and equally sad results. Ordinarily, the short pitch I needed to hit traveled two to three times as far as required. Occasionally, however, I was rethinking the force that I had decided upon as the clubhead approached the ball, and this caused me to decelerate as I hit it (or to stop entirely), causing me to hit what is commonly referred to as a chili dip (a ridiculous, yet strangely appropriate term which is spelled as one word in Texas, I believe).

I also compounded my short game woes by ignoring all of the advice contained in golf magazines, deciding to use only one club for all of my short game needs. It's a wonderful little midwedge (God, but I do love golf terminology) that I picked up for fifteen bucks some years ago, and it was so unusual looking that I fell in love with it immediately. Unfortunately, as any good player could tell me, this club was not capable of doing all of the things I wanted it to do, despite its pleasing appearance.

I *knew* this, of course. Many shots around the green call for a club with less loft, but I had created a system that was supposed to compensate for different lies, slopes, and trajectories. When I wished to hit a pitch and run, for example, I turned the club a bit in my hands, decreasing its loft. Similarly, when I wanted to hit a high shot, I opened the club face to increase the loft. This might have been called a creative approach, if a player were allowed only three or four clubs in his bag. In practice, however, I had all sorts of trouble adjusting the loft of the club to the distance I desired. Still, I stuck to my little midwedge, because I told myself that it made my golfing life less complicated. The result, of course, is that I made the game even more complex and difficult than it already is.

Good players realize that the short game is ever more important to good scores than the full shots. That's why they spend so much time on it. They actually wish to make their golf less complicated and they score better as a result.

It's really quite simple, but a lot of players never seem to learn. They spend most, if not all, of their precious practice time on one facet of the game, the one that has the least to do with becoming good players (or at least players who can win a five dollar bet on the last hole with a lengthy putt or a good up and down). It's not exactly a great mystery. Everyone knows that the short game is the key, but the vast majority of players fail to spend the time required to improve it. Instead, they take what they've been trying to do on the range and apply it to every challenge that the game presents them.

If golf consisted solely of determining who hits the ball the farthest, then perhaps I could justify the practice routine I followed. But since the object of the game is to take the fewest strokes possible, anyone who wants to become better *must* spend a great deal of time on the short game. In other words, good scoring demands subtlety and creativity rather than power or brute force. Poorer players may talk about how important the short game is, but they only say it as they walk past the practice green on their way to the range. And they only resolve to change their ways when the short game has cost them several strokes (or several dollars) during a round. Such a desire typically lasts only as long as it takes them to get back out there to the range, where they can really let loose. I know. I'm a recovering practice range addict.

Good players have astonishingly creative short games. I once saw someone (Johnny Miller, I think) hit a sand shot *away* from the green, bouncing it off of some of those railroad ties that Pete Dye likes to use, because he couldn't make a pass at the ball in the conventional, toward-the-hole fashion. He got up and down, too, as I recall. I've also seen Greg Norman chip with a three wood, and I once watched as Fred Couples actually turned his putter ninety degrees and hit it with the toe of the club when he had an incredibly fast shot out of deep grass around the green. How do they come up with such ideas? I suppose it's because they try to imagine the trouble that the game can present and then do what they can to prepare for it, or because they have encountered similar difficulties in the past and have decided, wonder of wonders, to be prepared to increase their chances for success the next time they occur. My approach to the game did not, unfortunately, allow me either to anticipate or to learn from my troubles.

My golfing life has often consisted of a refusal to absorb any of the important lessons that the game teaches. Among them is the understanding that it's wise to pay attention to the little things. Face it, all of those subtle, dippy little shots add up in a hurry. They may not seem like much as they are happening, but they all count when we put a number on the scorecard. How many times do we reach the fringe in two and then take six because we cannot imagine (or pull off) a shot that will work for us? The occasional good drive may console us after we make double bogie, but it cannot change our score for the better all by itself.

If I applied my old practice routine to life in general, it was as if I expected each day to present me with some Herculean task, some heroic effort like snatching a child from the path of oncoming traffic. In reality, my life, like that of everyone else, consists mainly of little encounters that don't seem to mean much at the time but turn out to be incredibly important. I sometimes wonder if players with great short games are better than other people at dealing creatively with the countless little situations that arise in, say, their relationships with their children. Maybe so, maybe not; but the deft touch that they use on the golf course certainly indicates that they appreciate this important fact of life, at least in theory.

Golfers are allowed to carry fourteen different clubs in their bags. This indicates (if a person wishes to learn) that golf teaches another important lesson: not every situation is the same, and different shots require different approaches and different tools. But even more than that, good players recognize that their clubs may be used in ways no one else ever dreamed of. Such creativity comes through practice. But players must first know that they *need* to practice.

Whether we are pros or not, golf allows us to carry fourteen clubs of our own choosing. In other words, we have the tools that we need, but it's up to us to recognize their potential, to make use of them when various occasions arise. When I was out there on the range, I ignored the short game, certainly, but I also saw the clubs I *did* practice with in one dimension. A five iron was the club to use when I was 170 yards or so from the green, for example. It only occurred to me that it could come in handy when I was faced with a delicate shot that needed to stay low to the ground when I actually had to *use* it that way. But because I didn't practice doing this, I faced such a shot with much more anxiety than it deserved.

It was the same in other areas of my life. I have a pretty fair sense of humor, a gift which often displays itself in understatement, but I used to squander opportunities to use it. Instead of a gentle comment (aimed at myself or someone else) that might bring a healthy perspective to a tense moment, I often resorted to a blast of sarcasm. I tended to flail away, full steam ahead, in all situations, rather than to survey the lay of the land, looking for another approach that might be preferable. When I did this, I damaged myself and other people by expecting too much (and saying so). I believed so passionately in power that I failed to recognize my limits, especially when I knew that a lot was on the line. It's no wonder I had a terrible short game. I often had no idea when subtlety was called for.

This was no surprise, actually. My game was much like my life. Though I told myself I had everything necessary to deepen my relationships, I rarely made use of the gentler gifts at my disposal. I avoided thinking about encounters that had caused me pain or confusion in the past, rather than trying to learn from them and to be prepared when they happened again. And when I was really in trouble, I fell back on the big guns, looking for scapegoats or trying to bluff my way through difficult situations. It was sad, and, worse, it was unnecessary.

When I was out there on the practice tee, blasting away, I was simply following a pattern that had brought me more than my share of unnecessary trouble, both on and off the course. In the long run, I would have benefited greatly from a little time spent on the short game. Such a routine might also have presented me with an image of a different approach to relationships with people, namely, that a little subtlety goes a long way, much farther, in fact, than those monster drives I dreamed of hitting.

Nowadays, when you think of monster drives, John Daly is the person who comes to mind. I once saw him play at a pro/celebrity tournament, and *everyone* was following him, shouting out encouragement and exhorting him to "grip it and rip it," to swing away and hit the ball a mile or two. And he didn't disappoint. When he teed the ball up on a long par five, his shot traveled over three hundred yards and also followed the contours of the hole, gently drawing as the fairway moved from right to left. The shouts of approval and the disbelieving shakes of people's heads indicated that the crowd got what it had been looking for.

Ever since his arrival at the 1991 PGA tournament, Daly has been a story. Often as not, however, the story has been about his reckless or outrageous behavior rather than about his huge shots. Even casual observers of the game know about his alcoholism, his drunken brawls, and other assorted disasters. In lots of ways, his behavior has attracted the same kind of attention that his drives have won for him. They are impossible not to watch, because they go so far and because they might just wind up anywhere. In other words, he seems to attack the golf ball and the course with the same kind of abandon that he brings to his personal life, and the results often get him into trouble. If you "grip it and rip it" in life, you are probably going to have to do a lot of apologizing or at least be prepared to make a few excuses.

Daly said something during that little pro/celebrity event which sounded like the equivalent of swinging away. The remark came as he prepared to hit his approach to the sixth green. He had hit a one iron from the tee to within about forty yards on a very long par four, and because I was still trying to take this in, I almost missed his comment. As he reached for a wedge, he said, loudly enough for people in his vicinity to hear, "Since I quit drinking, I can't see straight." Everyone who heard it laughed, of course, and Daly hit the shot and walked on. But as I recalled the comment later, two thoughts came to mind.

In the first place, I suspect that he uses this line a lot. It is certainly a crowd pleaser. In fact, I heard him make a similar comment as I was watching a tournament on TV some weeks later. A person might conclude that he was simply engaging in a little showmanship, that he was just trying to please the crowds that can't seem to get enough of him. Maybe so, but I also found myself wondering if this statement indicates the way he is approaching his ongoing recovery.

Of course, Daly cannot deny that he is an alcoholic. The newspaper stories preceding his going into treatment were printed all over the world. When he returned to the tour, he knew that many of the people watching him were like the folks who slow down as they pass a wreck on the highway. If they were not actually taking bets as to how long he'd last before he went back to the bottle, many of them likely assumed that his history would eventually catch up with him and that he would find other ways to flame out or self-destruct. And since his return, there *have* been times when he has attracted negative attention by doing or saying something impulsive. In other words, his life often winds up in the rough, just like some of those monster drives.

That, of course, is why his little offhand comment during the celebrity event said so much about him. Though it might well have included a desire to please the crowd, it might also have been another in a never-ending series of reminders to himself. He is, and always will be, a recovering person. As difficult as that is, he is also a public person, one whose mishaps have been screamed from the mastheads of major newspapers. Recovery is difficult under the best of circumstances, but most recovering persons are known to be so by a relative few, and they are often pledged to secrecy. Daly might as well walk around with a sign on his back: "I'm a drunk."

So when he made his crowd-pleasing comment, he might also have been engaging in a little therapeutic exercise, another reminder to himself that though he cannot deny his past, being honest about it may help him to avoid repeating it. A cynic could say that he might as well admit what everybody knows anyway, but a cynic would also have to admit that he doesn't know what it takes to get into recovery and to continue on that road, particularly when you are a public person. Daly knows, as few others do, how difficult life becomes when perfect strangers can quote press stories that reveal your darkest side, your biggest mistakes, the shame-filled episodes of your life. Recovery depends upon facing that shame head on so as not to be crushed by it.

Thus, Daly's comment may say a lot about who he is and about who is trying to be. Just as he steps up to the ball and swings away, he is facing his demons, or at least trying to do so. He is honest about his past as he attempts to move beyond it. He knows that he will get nowhere, and fast, if he tries to pretend that the past didn't happen. In the meantime, he still manages to hit it into trouble occasionally. Some of his escapades since treatment indicate that well enough. It seems a part of his nature to swing away. Sometimes, a person has to fall back upon strength.

On the other hand, there's a balance which life requires. Though we must sometimes bring all of the strength we can gather to face various challenges, life also demands a soft touch, a creative approach, an understanding of which battles are worth fighting (as well as how to fight them) and which ones should be avoided. In other words, life demands a good short game as well as the occasional use of power. And the truth is that John Daly has both. About a month after I saw him play in that pro/celebrity event, he won the British Open, and that victory underscored both the need for a short game and Daly's seeming ambivalence toward it.

Sunday afternoon at St. Andrews provided the viewer with as stark a contrast as is possible in golf these days. As Daly reached the sixteenth tee, Jack Nicklaus himself was offering commentary from the booth. Just as Nicklaus said that Daly would be better off asking someone in the crowd to hold his driver and not to return it to him until he had left the eighteenth tee, Daly reached for the driver and ripped away. Nicklaus couldn't keep from groaning when he saw it, and he kept coming back to his opinion that Daly could only cause himself trouble by trying to force the issue. If he could exhibit even a little patience and restraint, he could win the tournament, but if he insisted upon swinging away, he could easily lose what might be his best chance to win the British Open (because St. Andrews is so forgiving of errant shots).

He had a point, of course. Every time that Nicklaus opens his mouth to talk about golf, people should listen up. He's earned that kind of respect. And Nicklaus wasn't talking about being cautious so much as he was urging Daly to be sensible. Discretion is the better part of valor, and so on. I found myself agreeing with him (I'm not a total fool). But then neither I nor Nicklaus is John Daly. So he let loose and blasted the ball all the way back to the clubhouse.

When Constantino Rocca, his nearest competitor, chunked his pitch shot on eighteen, it appeared that Daly had survived despite his refusal to gear down a little. But then he sank an impossible putt through the entire length of the "valley of sin" to force the four hole playoff which, among other things, distinguishes the British Open from other major tournaments. The way I saw it, however, Rocca was finished before it even began, because he had expended so much emotional energy on eighteen and because he was facing so much power.

During the playoff, however, it was Daly's short game that carried him through. He hit a wonderful and daring pitch to the first green, and he sank a long and difficult putt on the second hole. By the time that Rocca hit his approach to seventeen into the road hole bunker, he was finished, but only because Daly had hit an exquisite approach with a short iron after another monster drive (ill-advised, as Jack said from the booth). But Nicklaus had also been commenting on Daly's wonderful short game throughout the broadcast. He had rightly pointed out that Long John's putting, chipping, and sand play had kept him in the tournament even when his errant tee shots had threatened to destroy any chance he might have had.

Daly's short game *is* marvelous, but it gets very little attention from the crowds who follow him. For the most part, they want him to keep hitting it a mile, and consequences be damned. A year or so ago, when he won in Atlanta, everyone talked about his two huge shots on eighteen, but it was his delicate little up and down from a greenside bunker that secured the win. Time and again, this man with a reputation for power relies on his short game to get him out of the trouble that his power gets him into; but he also uses it to take advantage of situations which his power provides him.

I suppose that Jack Nicklaus was trying to make a couple of points as he commented on Daly's short game that afternoon. In the first place, I think he was urging Daly to believe in his short game enough to make more use of it. If he could learn to trust it a bit more, and if he could try to rein in all of that power that the crowds like so much, he might experience more success on tour. After all, Daly has a short game that virtually anyone could envy. On the other hand, Nicklaus seemed to be saying that Daly takes his short game so much for granted that he ends up putting more pressure on it than it can sometimes bear. If you constantly have to hole eight footers for par, or if your short game can do nothing for you but help you to get up and down, it will eventually break under the strain.

Some would call Jack Nicklaus overly cautious, but even if this is so, he has come by that caution honestly. I vividly remember a tournament he lost early in his career because he pulled out his driver on the eighteenth tee and promptly jacked it a mile left out of bounds, even though he was leading at the time. Back then, many people failed to appreciate him because he had dethroned their beloved Arnold, but they still marveled at his power. Maybe *he* thought too much of his power back then, just as Daly seems to do. Anyway, as a result of his experiences, Nicklaus has gained a healthy respect for the danger that swinging away can bring, as well as for its usefulness.

The need for a balance between strength and subtlety in life, and in golf, is a constant. Thus, knowing which is called for is among the most important elements in a life well lived or a game well played. If a player stands on a tee and sees that the fairway narrows considerably in the landing area, he is well advised to use a club that avoids the possibility of a big mistake. This is analogous to the choices a parent faces when a child gets himself into trouble. Many such events call for a balance of power and touch, a combination of restriction (like the temporary loss of privileges) and understanding (acknowledgment of the child's need to rebound from the incident). When parents scream and yell about abused trust, they may satisfy their own desire to gain control, but they also run the risk of increasing the child's sense that he or she (rather than their behavior) is unacceptable. A softer touch could help children to see that they are loved enough to admit their mistakes. Strength and subtlety can accomplish more in tandem than either of them can do alone.

During the playoff, the seventeenth hole displayed what can happen for Daly under the best of circumstances. He hit his driver, of course, but he hit it so long and so far left that he was able to hit that great iron. It landed short and then followed the shape of the green, coming to rest safely and assuring him of a two putt par. Both power and touch came into play, and they worked together beautifully. It was wonderful to see.

But Nicklaus' points were well taken. Why would Daly take the chance of throwing away the tournament by hitting a driver when a smaller club could put him safely on the fairway and take some of the pressure off his short game? Only Daly could answer that, and I suspect that though he didn't seem to hesitate in choosing a club, he might be at pains to explain himself.

Perhaps he was going with what had brought him all of that adulation in the first place. After all, the crowds don't follow him because he chooses to play it safe. People still like to drive by those accidents slowly, taking a good long look. And Daly seems to get energy from the crowds who urge him on. Maybe he's trying to live up to a reputation, even when he's not so sure it's good for him to do so. After all, he already tends to go full throttle all of the time, and the crowds who scream for him to rip away may encourage him to take unnecessary chances, even when his better instincts are trying to offer him alternatives. In other words, the crowds are a gift, but one that may hurt, as well as help, him. Maybe he does it for the same reason he made that comment I heard at the pro/celebrity event. If he faces his troubles straight on and doesn't back off from them, he will eventually stare the demons down.

But maybe he _does_ take his short game for granted and, in

doing so, maybe he puts needless strain on that gift by asking it to make up for too many errant full shots. Perhaps he'd be better off if he thought so highly of it that he planned ahead a little more often so that he could bring it into play. I suspect he understands this better than most people, even if he tends to blast away when he's on the course.

It's one thing to stare the demons down; it's quite another to invite them in when they are at the door. I suspect, for example, that Daly does his best to stay away from places and circumstances which would tempt him to drink. It's the sensible thing to do. And if he is having a bad day, he probably knows that he has recovering friends in whom he can confide. These are little touches, but they are extremely important ones. A balance between power and the gentle approach will help him stay sober, as few of his fans could appreciate. When he's away from the course, I hope he looks for that balance.

John Daly can hit it a mile, and he can devise all sorts of creative little shots to get him out of trouble and to take advantage of the opportunities that his long game sometimes gives him. His golfing history appears to indicate, however, that he'd benefit from the balance which Nicklaus talked about. Above all, Nicklaus seemed to be saying that people ought to use all of their gifts, especially since the gifts are rationed so sparingly. When someone like Daly comes along, both he and the people who watch him can be so bowled over by the power that they fail to recognize the importance of the soft touch. As we all know, people did the same with Nicklaus, and he talks as if the expectations of the crowd sometimes led him to reach beyond his grasp, even when he knew better. Keeping that balance is difficult, no matter where we are.

To some degree or other, all of us *know* better than to rely upon power alone. All of us *know* that we have a variety of gifts, and that, just like the different clubs in a golf bag, they are there for a reason. But we allow ourselves to be so captivated by power that we rely upon it far too much. We become so enamored of strength that we try to use it in every situation, even when a closer look would tell us that a different approach might well do the trick. The greatest danger is that if we ignore the gentler approach, we might lose the ability to know when and how it can help us.

All human relationships demand a balance much like that between full shots and the short game. A parent obviously doesn't have the luxury of time when a small child is about to run into the street, and a little pop on the butt to get the child's attention can go a long way. On the other hand, the best parents I know are the ones who realize that being gentle and understanding can accomplish a lot more than a full-throated rant and rave. Sometimes we must confront our friends if they are headed in a dangerous direction or if they have hurt us, knowingly or not. But we must also be able to forgive, to prove our love for people by having compassion even as we are being as honest as we can.

Practicing the short game once seemed so boring to me that I rarely did it. Then, when I was actually playing a round of golf, the score mounted up because I hadn't nurtured the skills that would save strokes in all of those little situations that require creativity and a soft touch.

It was the same with my life. I spent all of my time preparing for the big moments that hardly ever arrived, scarcely aware that all of the little moments, each of which seemed so insignificant, added up and eventually defined me.

I'm not sure how it was decided that a player could carry no more than fourteen clubs in a golf bag. It's a mystery, I suppose. But the greater mystery by far is just how we get the gifts that we all possess. They differ from person to person, but one constant remains. Though their use is up to us, all of them can be employed in a variety of ways, depending upon the need of the moment. Golf has helped me to understand that.

6

UP AND DOWN

Like a lot of average golfers, I take pleasure in playing eighteen holes or so with someone who is not as good as I am. Unfortunately, it is sometimes difficult to find such a creature, since most of those who are worse than I am have already been snatched up by other players of my caliber. So when I find someone who plays very poorly, I quickly jump at the chance to go to the course.

This practice has provided me with many memorable games, a fair number of snagged clothes (as we look for lost balls in the woods), and an increase in my ability to display compassion. But it has also brought me face to face with some awkward truths about myself, many of which I'd rather not be reminded of.

One June day, I stumbled upon a threesome who asked me to join them. I was wary, since I might unwittingly be agreeing to play with three low handicappers. But it was a seldom-used public course, and I decided that the odds of all three being good players were slim. As we teed off, I discovered that I had presumed correctly.

The first two guys dribbled their drives as far as the ladies' tee, and the third one missed the ball entirely on his first try. Immediately, I knew two things: the round was probably going to last a bit longer than usual, but my chances of being embarrassed were about one in a thousand. When my drive bounded into the fairway and then rolled to the one-fifty marker (it was a short par four), my playing companions looked at me with respect. It appeared that I was going to get a lot of practice at being low-key about my obvious (but relative) skills.

I was prepared to say encouraging things to them, but I didn't realize that this would be considerably more difficult than usual. After all, what can you say when a player misses the ball completely or manages to knock it sideways? After these sorts of things had happened numerous times, I decided that silence was probably the best strategy. Each time that one of them apologized for holding me up or for standing in the line of my putt, I would say, "No problem," but I would also feel a stab of guilt, because I had long ago given up trying to be helpful or compassionate and was now secretly trying to find some graceful way to separate myself from them at the turn.

But they were so gracious that this was not going to be easy. I found myself wishing that at least one of them would do something obnoxious or would otherwise give me an excuse to quit the group. But they were unfailingly polite and solicitous of my feelings. They had also become a sort of cheering section. As I prepared to hit a shot, they all observed me closely, and they praised my play relentlessly. Even when I was unhappy with one of my shots, they complimented me; even my worst shots were better than theirs by far.

My thoughts grew nastier with each passing hole, and my guilt increased because my own unkind thoughts were such a contrast to all of their gracious ones. If even one of them had talked during my backswing or made a snide comment about how I must have plenty of leisure time in which to sharpen my game, I could have justified all of my interior complaints and felt better about abandoning them. But they wouldn't cooperate; instead, they became even nicer. When we approached a concession stand, they bought me a drink, despite my protests. It was the least they could do, they said, because I had been so patient with them. Had they only known.

Of course, this internal conflict had to affect my game eventually. As I entertained all of those mean-spirited thoughts, my concentration began to wane. Soon, I was playing in my usual erratic way. Finally, I topped a shot into a bunker, and they began to sympathize with *me*. One of them said that their poor play was beginning to rub off on me. He was sorry that this had happened. But I felt compelled to say that this was not the case, and I had to say it convincingly, because it was exactly what I had been thinking.

It was not, however, exactly what I had been looking for when I had agreed to join the group. I had hoped that I would get a cheap thrill or two, that my game would appear to be wonderful in comparison to theirs. Now that I had played back toward their level, my only defense was to blame them for it. These thoughts had to remain secret, however, because part of the cheap thrill came from having sympathy for them. You know, the good player being gracious and refusing to complain or become impatient with those who are not up to his standards.

Clearly, I had been trying to juggle two mutually exclusive desires. In the first place, I wanted these guys to see me as a good player, not simply one who was better than they were. As long as my shots surpassed any that they could manage, I could believe this. But when I played a poor shot, I needed to blame them for it, so that I could maintain the illusion that I was the player I want to be. I wanted it both ways: to be responsible for anything good I did, but to find a scapegoat when I did something wrong.

Worse yet, I couldn't even manage to be patient with players who weren't as good as I was. This in itself proved that I was not the sort of player I desired to be. I recalled that I had been in my playing companions' shoes from time to time. Whenever I had played with people who really were good, they had been infinitely patient and understanding with me. They had never given any clues that they were exasperated or looked for excuses to leave me behind at the turn. As far as I knew, they had never entertained any of the callous thoughts that filled my head as I played with these three novices.

If I were really going to be honest, I'd have to admit that I had much more in common with my playing companions that day than I did with good players. Yet I spent all of my time that afternoon distancing myself from them, telling myself that I was much better than they were, even as I found it increasingly difficult to sustain these fantasies.

This was a perfect example of self-righteousness, an attitude that feeds off the imperfections of others as a means of denying imperfections in oneself. Because I was a moderately better player than they were, I could see myself as a great player by comparison with them. At least I could do this as long as I played better than they did. When I began to play like them, I had to blame them for my mistakes if I were going to continue to live with the delusions that I had created.

If I had tried to develop such an attitude on the golf course, I would have failed miserably, as that afternoon's round proved. Instead, I found that a practice I had learned and perfected in other areas of my life couldn't survive on the course. It was simply too difficult to maintain the illusion when there was such clear evidence against it.

I had never thought of golf as an antidote to self-righteousness, but I changed my mind that afternoon. If you play the game for any length of time, you discover that it is far too spiritual to support as false a notion as pride for very long. If you take what the game gives you and refuse to manipulate the figures, you will benefit in ways that you never dreamed possible. I'm a lot less self-righteous these days because I play inconsistent golf, and because I ran into three even poorer players by chance one afternoon. It's enough to make me believe that there are no accidents.

You don't have to be the player I am to find that golf can slap you down, rid you of some of the pretensions that you have accumulated, and at least attempt to teach you a thing or two about yourself and life in general.

The year the U.S. Amateur was played at the Honors Course in Chattanooga, I went to watch. Phil Mickelson was still an amateur then, and I expected that he and a few other people (Jay Sigel, for example) would impress me quite a bit. But I didn't know what I was talking about. They could *all* hit it, and most of them had great short games, too. Everywhere I looked, I saw people who had what I would call complete games. Yet only sixty-four of them made it through the first two rounds of medal play. The rest of those very good players were sent home without a chance to go for the big prize.

If you attend a tournament on the PGA, LPGA, Nike, or other tours, you quickly see that all of *them* can play, too, even better than the average player who qualifies for the Amateur. As everyone knows, the competition is fierce. A number of players may survive, but only a relative few achieve a level of success that rids them of financial worries for a lifetime and assures their place in the history of the game.

Since everybody at that level can play, the people who consistently finish high on the money list clearly have something that the others don't. And it's not just luck or skill. It can't be, because the skills are more or less even, and all of them get a good break once in a while. I also doubt that it's desire, since nobody gets to that level without a lot of that commodity. Regardless what it might be, I think that people like me fail to understand something important when we try to figure out the extra element in the people who find success. It's likely that the players we admire are meditating upon something else altogether.

When you hear a truly great player talk about himself or herself, you may get the idea that he or she is holding back out of modesty. Jack Nicklaus, for example, likes to say that he has experienced "a measure" of success in golf. The understatement of the century, at least in sports. I suspect, however, that he is not being modest at all, or, if he *is*, it's because golf has taught him not to boast. No one masters the game; it will break your heart if you are foolish enough to think you've figured it out. And it may break your heart even if you are trying to remain free of pretension.

I recall hearing a commentator talking about a particularly disastrous round of golf by Nicklaus during the British Open one year. He had shot an 84 or something horrible like that, and the sportscaster said that after years of wishing that he played like Nicklaus, now he could say that he did. Jack had come back to this man's level of play. There was a lot of irony in this cute little statement, and I suppose that the man complimented himself for his cleverness. But I wonder what Nicklaus thought about it. Even though he might have harbored a nasty thought or two about the comment (the sportscaster never had his scores published in the world press), I suspect that he took it all as yet another reminder that no one, not even he, can say that he has arrived.

Clearly, Nicklaus has experienced more success in tournament golf than anyone of his time. Virtually everyone refers to him as the best who's ever played the game, and that's very likely true. Yet *because* of all his success, he has probably experienced more disappointment than anyone else, too. Precisely because he has had so much success, he knows better than anyone else that the game itself is the only master. We might all wish that we played like him, but if we entertain those dreams, they represent a certain lack of understanding on our part. When we harbor those thoughts, we are, in our naiveté, expressing a desire to get a handle on the game. Nicklaus knows, as perhaps no one else does, that this is a fantasy. In other words, the better a player's game gets, the deeper becomes his appreciation for what he can't achieve. This is an extremely spiritual understanding. Mystery is ultimately impenetrable.

I suppose that players like me look at the great ones and think that all of our troubles would be over if we could simply hit it like they do. We've experienced so much frustration on the course that people like Nicklaus seem to have it made. We forget that they have many of the same experiences that we do, albeit on a somewhat more elevated level. When Nicklaus shanked that ball off the twelfth tee at Augusta in 1995, I couldn't believe what I was seeing. Now *I* played like Nicklaus. But he had good reason to turn to the crowd and to tell the people that he had done it once before on the same hole. It was about thirty years ago, but he remembered it like it was yesterday. Golf had taught him to have as good a memory for the lows as the highs. This is a wonderfully effective method for shooting down pride whenever it appears on the horizon.

That's one of the great benefits golf offers. Even the best players are a momentary lapse of concentration from failure. As long as they know this, they will focus on their games instead of entertaining thoughts about how few players are as good as they are. No matter how often they've won or otherwise been at the top of their games, they can lose it just like the weekend scrub. When Jack hit that shank, it occurred to me that even though he probably felt somewhat embarrassed by it, the people watching him felt it a lot more than he did. You could hear it in the crowd. There was a surprised gasp, then an unbelieving silence. It was as if the folks in the crowd thought that this was a major disaster. Nicklaus knew better.

Really good players have the opportunity to experience something that lesser players cannot even imagine (and find hard to believe). Not only is it true that no one masters the game, but those who try to do so are bound to fail. The more we are capable of doing, the more we realize that the game is beyond us. That, I think, is why Nicklaus talks about having achieved a "measure" of success at the game. To the rest of us poor slobs, he's a god, but he knows that he stands at the mercy of the game every bit as much as we do. Humility is the proper stance when you are in the presence of mystery.

People who play good golf are probably the most modest of athletes, and for good reason. Though they must work very hard to achieve that measure of success, though the hours of practice are endless, though the degree of concentration must be intense, they know, as few other athletes know, that they can take only so much credit for what they achieve. And I'm not talking about the athletes who thank God for their success, as if God really spent any time at all being concerned about who won the Super Bowl. No, it's a purer form of modesty, one which acknowledges that their gifts are just that: talents for which they can take only a finite amount of credit.

Once in a great while, I hit a great shot. When this happens, I am filled with a feeling that is difficult to describe. I know only that I like the experience enough to wish it would happen a bit more often. There's a part of me that believes I *can* do it, maybe not all of the time, but often enough that my scores would improve. More important, a part of me *wants* desperately to do it. If I could only hit shots like that more often . . .

But a number of things get in the way. I am not willing to put in the time it takes, and even if I am, I'm not willing to submit to someone who can help me to get where I want to go. I'd much rather get there myself, because then I could take the credit. If I were in Nicklaus' shoes, I'd certainly find a way to remind everyone, on a more or less constant basis, about all of my triumphs.

But I'm not in his shoes, however, and I can only wonder at the way he talks about himself. At times, I tell myself that he has to feign modesty after all that he has achieved. But his words are so authentic that I soon reject that thought. It's not that he doesn't think his achievements are a big deal, because clearly they are. Instead, I like to think he knows that though he developed the talent he was born with, he didn't simply wish his gifts upon himself. Even though he has used them spectacularly well and gotten more out of them than others might have, none of this started with him.

Despite the hard work, the hours of practice, the countless lessons, everything that has come his way is a gift. And he's gotten far enough to understand that even the disappointments are gifts, too, because they remind him not to get so caught up in himself that he forgets who he is: another person struggling to make use of what he's been given, trying to remember always that success is dangerous if it leads him to see himself as somehow better or more deserving than the next guy.

It's funny and sad that I would take delight in playing eighteen holes with some poor player who is even worse than I am because it gives me a rare opportunity to feel just a little bit superior to someone. Nicklaus, who until recently couldn't help but feel superior to *anyone* he played with, wouldn't dream of taking such advantage, even secretly. I bet that he's much less likely to be filled with self-righteousness now than he was thirty-five years or so ago. I'd also wager that golf has had a lot to do with his attitudes toward himself and everyone else. It's that kind of game.

Pride and self-righteousness are the deadliest of attitudes because they allow us to delude ourselves into believing all sorts of nonsense. And while all of those beliefs tend to distance us from other people, they eventually lead us to the deadliest conclusion of all: the belief that we have arrived, that we have nothing else to learn or to give. Other people might have to keep working at developing themselves, but we are just fine, thank you.

Of course, good players can become just as prideful as anyone else, but I imagine that it's a struggle. People who play golf and are honest about what they shoot are forced to admit, at one time or another, that there is no such thing as reaching, or even defining, the ultimate goal, no matter how successful they get. The temptation to stop working on ourselves always exists, but golf has a way of bringing a person back down to earth with the rest of humanity. Truly fortunate people know, at least within themselves, that pride can only be rooted out by gratitude, the awareness that everything is a gift which must be used wisely. All gifts are given to us so that we can find our way to ourselves and to the One who gave us the gifts in the first place. Golf is always ready to remind us of that. We only need to pay attention.

Sometimes, even when we're not paying attention or would rather not have to learn the lesson, golf, like life, insists that we listen up. This is as true for the weekend hacker as it is for the touring pro, but the pros have a more difficult time ignoring the message because they have the press acting as a sort of Greek chorus for them.

God only knows how many words have been written about Greg Norman's "failures" in major tournaments, but the number certainly increased after the 1996 Masters. Even people who follow golf in the most tentative of ways are aware of the stories.

Until 1996, the two most famous ones involved impossible shots by players who were down to their proverbial last gasps. Larry Mize had hit his second far right of the green during a playoff for the Masters, and Bob Tway was in the bunker at eighteen in the last round of the PGA. Each of them had difficult up and downs, and both of them holed their shots. In each case, Norman was just a few minutes away from taking home one of the major tournaments. In both cases, he went home empty-handed. And these are not the only majors Norman has lost on the last day or last hole, as everyone who follows golf knows.

After the 1996 Masters, people who don't follow the

game, even people who don't much *like* the game, must know of Norman's most recent disaster at Augusta. After tying the course record with a 63 on Thursday, he continued to play well, making putt after putt from one of the toughest positions in golf: the top of the leader board during the second week of April. For fifty-four holes, he threatened to make Sunday's telecast a ho-hum, try-to-find-something-to-say-from-the-tower sort of day. But a combination of Nick Faldo's great shots and Norman's poor ones turned the final round into the prelude of yet another series of Greg Norman stories in the press. Before, during, and after the majors these days, Norman is the hot topic of people's speculations and pseudo-psychoanalysis. It's become a regular sideshow on the pro tour.

An awful lot of the writing about these events has centered on the rather slippery concept of fate. Norman is described as ill-fated, while his opponents are the darlings of fate. I suppose that these descriptions are almost inevitable, since many people see golf as a mirror or an image of life, and since many of life's events are difficult to explain or to understand, much like Norman's performances in some major tournaments. Many people, in and out of the press, have concluded that Norman has asked for the catastrophes he has experienced because he is so damned arrogant. In other words, these things couldn't have happened to a nicer guy. The arrogance angle has been around for some time.

Long before the 1996 Masters, people had written about a five-year plan that Norman had hatched. Most of what I read seemed to indicate that such a plan was presumptuous, even wildly so, given his record in the major tournaments. Nicklaus (in his prime) might be allowed a plan, but certainly not Norman. At least one writer said that Norman was tempting the same fate that had struck him down so often. In other words, he was fighting despair by becoming foolishly presumptuous. I tend to think, however, that both the despair and the presumption were in the mind of the writer.

Of course, presumption and despair can appear in golfers as in anyone else, but hope always exists as a middle road between these two deadly extremes. People who play golf are never far from an access road that leads to hope.

When I think about hope, presumption, and despair as they relate to golf, I remember the U.S. Open of 1966. I was a teenager then, a loyal member of Arnie's Army, and I was in heaven as he began the back nine on Sunday, seven shots "away from the field," as the British commentators like to say. But with each succeeding hole, my delirium faded, only to be replaced by a growing anxiety, which finally exploded into full-blown despair. Billy Casper, playing methodical golf, didn't so much overtake Palmer as he watched Arnold fall back toward him. When Palmer lost the playoff the next day, I wondered how I could have been so stupid as to think that he had it sewn up.

Like many people watching the tournament, I had committed the cardinal sin of presuming that the tournament was Palmer's for the taking. I didn't hope that he would win; I *knew* that he would. I needed only to wait an hour and a half or so and then watch him accept the trophy. As things got worse and worse for Arnold, I found that I couldn't hope that he would win. Presumption, when it is revealed for what it is, rarely moderates into hope; it usually rushes right past hope and becomes despair. This is especially true in golf. Anyone who has a favorite player or two has experienced the violent jolt which accompanies a dive from the penthouse of presumption to the basement of despair.

In spite of this, however, I believe that golf teaches people to steer toward the middle path of hope, and Greg Norman isn't the only example who comes to mind. In fact, when Mize and Tway made those winning shots, their victories became possible because they had refused to succumb to despair. Had they given up hope and simply gone through the motions, Norman might well have two more majors to his credit. To *their* credit, they continued to hope when virtually everyone else had pronounced them dead on arrival. And Nick Faldo, despite beginning the final round six shots behind, continued to play steadily spectacular golf, winning a tournament which everyone believed belonged to someone else.

Hope is always more difficult to generate in other sports. When a basketball team is down by twenty-five points, it takes more than a quick basket or two to inspire hope. And even if the losing team runs off fifteen unanswered points, it may be too early to entertain any dreams of victory. In baseball if the home team is down by six runs going into the bottom of the ninth, hope can only begin to have life if a couple of runs cross the plate and the tying run is at bat. Until then, hope is a bit too optimistic an inclination for all but the truest of believers (just check out the parking lot when the home team is down to its last out).

In golf, however, hope is never far from the surface, and even if it seems to be dashed by events, it may still make a comeback. This does not mean that presumption and despair can't make their appearance on the golf course (remember Arnie in 1966), and players at every level must battle against them; but golf, more than any other sport, promotes hope. This is never clearer than in the lives of average players. I should know.

My game can best be described as erratic. There have been rare occasions when I have fallen into presumption, days when I have been hitting the ball so well that I have routinely assumed that I could accomplish what I had hitherto been incapable of. On each of these occasions, however, I have finally come up against reality: I am not yet ready for the tour.

But I have had many more experiences of hope. Everyone who plays golf is familiar with the adage that any player, even in the midst of the most terrible round of his life, can hit one shot that will bring him back out again. It may be a good chip shot or a lucky bounce; it may take the form of the first ever up and down from a bunker or an unintentional fade that lands five feet from the pin. Regardless, any golfer can review a round and choose to believe that one good shot outweighs ninety bad ones. Even when reality seems to indicate that it would be prudent to give up, hope appears, and people go back out again.

If hope is an expectation that runs counter to the available evidence, then golf promotes hope far better than many other human activities. My game could easily sustain an attitude of despair, because my ratio of bad to good shots is so great. And I certainly know what it means to be filled with a conviction that my game is hopeless. Any number of times, I have left the course vowing never to return; more often, I have found myself ready to walk off after the next hole, if I can fake an injury or a bout of the flu.

When this has happened, I have been certain that I cannot play the game at all. This, in a nutshell, is what despair is all about. People in the midst of despair are *sure* that they have no reason to hope. In the same way, presumption is the *certainty* that hope is unnecessary; those who presume believe that they have everything under control. In other words, despair and presumption appear when people decide that the most recent evidence is *final.*

Despair is, of course, the greater enemy of players like me. But then, even when despair is deepest, I hit that one good shot, and hope suddenly makes its appearance. Maybe I *can* learn to play this game. Perhaps I *do* have what it takes to become a better player.

I don't know if Arnold Palmer ever presumed, at some point in that last round of that Open Tournament, that he would win. If he did, he probably also experienced the pain of despair afterward. That's the way it is with presumption and despair. They are interchangeable, and one always finds a way to become the other, because both arise when we are sucked into accepting the finality of some event. That's why the world needs golf as an antidote to these two dangerous enemies to our spirits. Any player, from Arnold to me, can find that hope is just one shot away.

Anyone who watched the 1996 Masters could see the anguish on Greg Norman's face as the tournament slipped away from him. As he approached the ninth tee, he was still well ahead, and he appeared to be quietly and firmly confident. But as he left the twelfth green, he trailed the man he was paired with. By the time he pulled his tee shot at sixteen into the water, he had nothing left to give or to hide.

Though he later insisted that his failure to win was not the end of the world, some of those who wrote about him hinted that he was blowing smoke, that he might never recover from such a disaster. Who could have faulted him if he had run away and hidden for a week or two? But he teed it up at Harbour Town the next week, playing on Hilton Head Island as if this were just another tournament, which is exactly what it was. Norman talked about getting back on the horse and all, and that's one way to describe what he was doing. But I think that his appearance at the very next tournament indicates that he refuses to be seduced by either presumption or despair.

A lot of people have called Greg Norman the victim of fate, whatever that is. And he may, at times, have believed this himself. But I'm willing to bet that he's learned a good deal about hope because of his near misses. Hope, after all, is not all that much about winning, even at the tournament level. It's about believing in one's *possibilities*, despite some evidence that achieving one's desires is an impossibility. Hope is always, before all else, about rejecting notions of finality.

This makes hope difficult to come by. We like easy answers, and we go on supplying them because complex answers demand greater effort and take us to mysterious places we'd often prefer to avoid. So we continue to define people, including ourselves, by adding up successes and failures, as if life were a balance sheet of some kind. But because defining people in this way is easy, it tells us very little. And because we make so much of success and failure, we find it difficult to experience the hope that we need. As we bounce back and forth between the extremes of presumption and despair, we are usually unaware that they have little to do with who we really are.

Anybody can give in to presumption and despair, and lots of folks remain in the grip of one or the other of them for long periods of time. But golf always seems to provide us with what we need to banish those two demons and replace them with hope.

The 1996 Masters is one in a series of experiences which could have caused Greg Norman to despair, just as his runaway triumph in the Players Championship in 1994 could have filled him to the teeth with presumption. But when he played the week after he lost to Faldo, he demonstrated that the five-year plan he launched some time back is based more upon hope than upon those two dangerous extremes. He also demonstrated that golf has taught him not to measure himself solely in terms of wins and losses. I think Norman has concluded that as long as he has hope, he takes something of value home with him every time he leaves the course. And he, like the rest of us, could use it.

Presumption and despair are troublesome enough on the golf course, but they are true spirit killers in the really important areas of our lives. Steering a middle course between those opposing but related extremes is vital if we are to experience any sense of fulfillment. When we realize that no evidence, however clear it appears to be, is the last word, we can pick ourselves up (or come down from the clouds) and get back to work. We can revive our hopes as long as we don't make too much of either our successes or our failures, as long as we remind ourselves that a measure of success is enough for anyone.

7

HAZARDS

I once read a letter to the editor in one of the golf magazines. The writer was commenting about a few profanities that Fred Couples had spoken aloud after hitting a shot during a tournament playoff some weeks before. He was not exactly pleased with his shot, as the comments he came out with indicated. The microphones that routinely follow the pros around the course had captured his words and broadcast them quite clearly to everyone who was watching, including me, as well as the irate letter writer.

The writer was displeased. He faulted Couples for what he had said, and complained that this sort of outburst was a bad example for younger players. Fred Couples and every other pro should be more conscious of the impact that they have on people, he said. If they couldn't control themselves on the course, how could younger players ever learn to do so? And so on.

The magazine had contacted Couples, and he had replied (through a spokesperson) that he was "embarrassed" by the incident. As it appeared in the magazine, his statement was a clear-cut apology that offered no excuses for his actions. I suppose he figured that damage control was the best he could do under the circumstances; he couldn't very well defend himself. But when I heard him say those words, I immediately found myself empathizing with him and feeling a bit better about myself. At last, Fred Couples and I had something in common.

When I took up golf in my teens, I had already added a rather complete list of profane words and phrases to my personal lexicon. The only additions since then have been some creative combinations which I wasn't experienced enough to compose (or to imagine) at the time. So I didn't learn to swear on the golf course. But that is where I learned to say those things *out loud*. Now I was pleased to discover that, just like Fred Couples, I could become upset on the course. And like him, I knew some very appropriate ways to express my frustration and displeasure.

As I read the letter and the response that day, I thought that most players (with the possible exception of Curtis Strange, whose comments are legendary) would find themselves "embarrassed" by a comment or two, if people with microphones followed them around all of the time. In fact, if people could read minds, many of *us* might find ourselves atoning for our "embarrassing" comments while spending a little time in the lock-up. In other words, Couples was taking the heat for all of us and apologizing for behavior that he shared with most people who have ever tried to play the game.

I realize, of course, that a lot of the pros manage to control themselves a little better than this. When Nicklaus says, "Oh, Jack," after hitting an errant shot, for example, I'm willing to bet that he is thinking something else. Given his stature, by the way, Nicklaus' name should regularly be invoked by high handicappers whenever the chance presents itself, though none of us should yell, "Oh, Jack," like he does. That would come dangerously close to taking "the name" in vain. Anyway, I suppose that Nicklaus, and other pros who behave likewise, deserve some credit for restraint.

In the long run, however, they are merely getting points for politeness. After all, profanity may be inappropriate in many contexts, but I'm not sure that it's all that big a deal. The taboos against certain expressions date from a time when people cursed each other only after careful consideration because they were literally trying to call upon the wrath of the Almighty. Nowadays, such expressions are more likely to be aimed at oneself. In Freddie's case, the words may have been ill-chosen (considering the presence of the microphones), but he really *was* swearing at himself, and his words certainly fit the context. Any player worth his salty language knows it, too.

The immediate context was the shot that brought the words to his lips. And Couples' comments, as I recall them, referred to the shot he had played. There was a bigger picture, however, and this is what added volume to his words and brought him all of that criticism.

He was in a playoff with Phil Mickelson, and his shot from the tee (a three wood, I recall) was a good one. As soon as he hit it, the commentator who was following the players remarked that it was "perfect." And it looked that way. As the ball sailed down the fairway, it was cutting a bit (his preferred play), but when it landed in the fairway, it bounced *left*, pretty much sideways into a bunker, coming to rest up against the lip. It shouldn't have happened; it almost *couldn't* have happened. He surely deserved better.

This was bad enough, but there was another element that added to the moment. Mickelson had been driving the ball poorly all afternoon, but *his* wild shots had usually resulted in good lies. He often hit the ball so far off the fairway, in fact, that he had an unobstructed view of the green. His poor shots had resulted in good breaks for him, and Fred's really good shot had resulted in disaster. It wasn't fair.

It's possible that all of this had gone through Couples' mind as he surveyed the shot. After all, he's only human (contrary to the opinions of some of the better young players I know). But as he stood over the ball, he knew that he could only work with what he had, break or no break. Unfortunately, what he had to work with was next to impossible. The best he could do was to blast the ball out as far as he could, knowing that it would take a miracle for him to reach the green (and none of this day's miracles had been going his way). When he skied the ball and it came up short, all of his frustration came to the surface. If I heard him correctly, he cursed himself because he was the logical target of his wrath. After all, he was the one who had failed to perform.

The letter writer allowed Fred's language to get in the way of his recognizing an important element in golf. When Couples uttered his now famous words, he was staring at mystery, and he was being reminded, as he had probably been reminded many times before, that doing everything right is no guarantee of success. He blamed himself because it was up to him to do what he could, but the result was really out of his hands. Something much bigger than he is had come into play, and despite his best efforts, he would not succeed.

The commentators working the tournament had been hinting at that all day, and it was all summed up in the anguished words that Couples had blurted out. He had played well, had hit his shots accurately, and his reward was an impossible sideways bounce into a trap. Mickelson had hit many poor shots, and his reward was a victory. It didn't make sense; it wasn't supposed to be that way. But one of life's mysteries had made its appearance, and its entrance was punctuated by a couple of remarks heard over TV sets around the country. The mystery in question was the nasty little fact that life is often unfair, a conclusion that human beings are so good at denying that they almost literally explode in anguish when it becomes impossible to ignore.

I suppose that I don't fault the wrathful letter writer. People should take care to watch what they say, and there are many circumstances that demand restraint. By complaining about Couples' language, however, he demonstrated that he had missed the most important component of the incident. Fred Couples was responding, as all human beings do, to the sudden and unmistakable realization that he was powerless in a fundamental sort of way. Things hadn't gone according to plan, despite some heroic efforts on his part, and there was nobody to blame (including himself, by the way). His words, ill-chosen though they might have been, were the twentieth-century equivalent of shaking one's fist at the heavens, crying out in vain for justice (or just a decent break). Sometimes it does no good to insist that we have done the best we can do and therefore deserve better.

I imagine that Couples spent some time reflecting on what happened that day. He may have played some of the shots over again in his mind, looking to learn from the experience. Then he probably did something that he appears to be good at: he put it behind him and went on (at least I hope he did). After all, the most appropriate response to powerlessness, after some well-chosen remarks, is acceptance. Powerlessness, after all, is not condemnation. It's a reminder that we are limited, that the world will not and cannot simply conform to our desires, no matter how desperate they are or how fiercely we try to make them come true.

It's interesting that a lot of the people who admire Fred Couples' game cannot forgive him for his ability to let go of the past. Maybe they so admire (or envy) his talent that they believe he should win everything, and if he doesn't, that he should look as if it kills him that he hasn't beaten the world every time that he goes out. On top of that, they expect him to watch his language. My guess is that such people don't handle *their* powerlessness very well either.

At one time or another, all human beings manage to fall into a particularly deadly trap: believing that if they want something, anything, badly enough, they should be able to achieve it. If the desire is great enough, people will run over anything or anybody in their path. Regardless, when reality sets in and people are forced to accept that their desires are beyond their ability to realize them, they are left with one of two equally unfortunate conclusions. Either they have failed because they have not tried hard enough, or there is no point in trying. All of us know people who consider themselves total failures because they could not achieve the impossible and others who have abandoned all attempts to achieve anything. Sometimes, we are those people; but it's somehow more difficult to acknowledge those frightening options when we see them in the mirror.

People usually bounce back from such depths, either to start the entire process all over again or perhaps (if they are lucky) to adjust their expectations of themselves and their understanding of the mysteries of life. Everybody would probably agree (in the abstract) that the best we can do is all we can do. The problem is that people tend to believe that they have done their best only when they have succeeded.

Golf presents people with countless opportunities to define the best they can do in other ways. Even people with a lot of game sometimes face situations that demand a little give. I've seen dozens of pros actually chip away from the pin because trying to aim for it will almost certainly result in a shot that runs through the green and into a lake or a bunker or God knows what kind of greater trouble. Usually, they have the good sense and the humility to take what the course gives them, instead of trying to force the issue and actually increasing their chances of a greater failure.

Then there are times like the one Fred Couples had in that tournament I've been speaking of. He was in a playoff, his opponent's ball was in better shape than his was, and there was nothing to do except to try for everything, even though the odds were against him. He failed, as he was almost bound to do, and his initial reaction was to assume the responsibility for that failure. But the feelings behind the words, and the depth of the anguish that they revealed indicated that circumstances beyond his control had landed him in a position that put success well beyond his reach. I sure hope he eventually came to that conclusion. I think it's the one that fits.

It is difficult to overstate what golf offers people regarding their ultimate powerlessness. While acceptance of one's powerlessness is vital, because it is one of the facts of life, one of the elements of the mystery, people routinely avoid facing it. You can hear this refusal whenever someone says, "I should have known," or "I must have missed something." If we listened to ourselves, we'd realize that we can only deny that we are powerless by expecting ourselves to do the impossible: to read people's minds or to predict the future, for example. Yet we find it much easier to expect ourselves to perform impossible feats than to accept that we are ultimately incapable of bending the world to our wills. Golf presents us with many opportunities to experience powerlessness when the stakes are relatively low. This is a blessing, if we are wise enough to accept it.

I think that golf instruction could benefit from analogies to other life situations, since the game so often mirrors other events in life. Like a lot of duffers, I read golf magazines, and I usually pay close attention to the lessons that they contain. At times the tips appear to be useful, even if some of the instruction is beyond my comprehension. But I know when I'm being had. The first clue that I'm buying snake oil is usually when the touring or teaching pro who is giving the lesson talks about how "easy" a particular shot is to execute.

Perhaps the most striking examples of this are the tips about playing from bunkers. On more than one occasion I have read that sand shots (at least around the green) are simple because the object is not to hit the ball. Pros seem to believe that we hackers will take comfort from this, but many of us can detect a not-so-subtle jab at our poor games. The instructors seem to think that since many of us mis-hit the ball a good bit of the time anyway, hitting out of traps should inspire no fear in us. When we're in the bunker, we can just swing away as we normally do, and if we miss the ball, the result will be a good shot. Just what we all need to hear, don't you think?

What the teachers don't seem to appreciate is that it is still necessary to miss the ball *precisely*. A miss that is too heavy will leave the ball in the trap, and one that is too thin will result in a bladed shot that sails over the green (and probably into the trap, lake, or woods on the opposite side). Every weekend player knows this.

Part of me recognizes that the people who talk about how easy the typical sand shot is really mean it; they are not condescending at all. And I've heard the on-course commentators say so often that a player feels lucky to have landed in the bunker that I think it before they say it these days. I know that *they* would rather be in sand traps than in heavy rough around the green, and I know all of the reasons. It's abundantly clear to me that they can usually get spin on the ball from a trap, while a ball in heavy grass will probably "fly" or "jump." None of this is helpful to me, however, because knowing it doesn't lessen the terror I feel when I land in a trap.

The easy-going attitude of the pros toward sand shots is in stark contrast to the fear with which the weekend player approaches them. Low handicappers simply don't get it. After reading about how to get up and down from a bunker, I am more likely to dread the next "opportunity" I have, because my lack of success has now been certified as a failure to master this supposedly simple aspect of the game.

Having said this, I must admit that I have occasionally managed to hit a pretty good shot from a sand trap. As often as not, however, my eyes have been closed at the time in order to prevent getting sand in them. While I might make some connection between closed eyes and good bunker shots, I know that this is not the way to increase the percentage of successful attempts. But then *trying* to miss the ball is not really going to help either. It's still necessary to miss the ball with precision, and this is not as easy as it might seem.

It's really a case of preferring the devil you know to the one you don't know, as they say. I'd much rather be in deep rough near a green than in a trap, because at least I'm familiar with that situation. If all greens were completely surrounded by sand, I'd probably see it differently, but very few courses that I know of are set up that way. Until they are, I'll take my chances with grass, regardless of its depth. While I realize that I won't be able to get the ball to do much, the chances of my at least advancing it are pretty good. And I rarely get the ball to "do much" (at least much that I *want* it to do) anyway. If I'm in a trap, I am automatically staring double bogey or worse in the face. When I'm on real land, I might actually hole the shot. It *could* happen.

It's no secret that I love to see a great player muff a sand shot. And the pleasure increases in direct proportion to the ease of the shot. While I know that this is mean-spirited on my part, I have to take what I can get. The problem is that good players are more likely to hole even a difficult sand shot than to hit anything that even vaguely resembles one of my efforts. Just when I get my hopes up, somebody like Paul Azinger holes a shot that everyone says he'd be lucky to get within ten feet. After the tournament, he's likely to say that the shot was actually a simple one. He may not have hoped to sink it, but he at least wanted to give it a chance. Thanks a lot, Paul.

I think it was 1992, and I turned on the TV just in time to see Fred Couples hit the ball out of a bunker on number sixteen at Augusta. As he hit the shot, his right hand came completely off the club, and I assumed that this was a mistake, because I've done this before myself, though not always on purpose. But then the ball trickled into the hole, and the commentator mentioned that Couples had been practicing this kind of shot for just such a situation.

This was not what I needed to hear. When I hit a sand shot, I hold the club so tightly that my hands might fuse themselves to it, such is my terror at the prospect of having to perform under the pressure that traps present to me. And here was Couples displaying the polar opposite in his approach to that vulnerable moment. You know sixteen at Augusta. If he had hit the ball with even a hint of velocity, his shot would have ended up at the bottom of the green (and it may have found the pond). It was a scary situation, and he responded by allowing one of his hands to come off of the club. He exerted less control, when the situation seemed to call for *more*. And because he tried for less control, he *got* more.

This, I think, sums up the difference between good and bad players when it comes to bunker play. Poor players feel frightened and vulnerable when they're in traps, so they grip harder, swing more wildly, and try desperately to control the events. Good players know that their chances of success actually increase if they're in the trap, that under most circumstances they can spin the ball in ways that they never could from the rough. So they relax and let the club and the sand work together.

Everyone, from the best pros to the rankest amateurs, has plenty of reason to feel vulnerable on the golf course. Whether it's a situation that confronts a person with feelings of powerlessness, like Fred Couples' experience in that playoff, a tough lie in a bunker, or a shot that is all carry over water, a player faces many shots that tend to raise the blood pressure, restrict breathing, or quicken the pulse. The pros know that tensing up or increasing the pressure on the grip, although it may be a natural response to vulnerability, is the exact opposite of what these situations really demand.

When I have to hit the ball over water, I usually think that I am being wise when I take an extra club. However, I then swing that one club more with four times more velocity than usual (and that's saying something), virtually assuring me of a shank or a topped shot or some other dreadful result. If I took that extra club and swung a bit easier (or at least if I tried to have an even tempo), I'd be more likely to reach the fairway or the green beyond the water that I worry so much about.

The same thing happens when I'm in one of those traps. I *know* what all of the instructors say, and I've seen the pros execute these shots many times, but my fears usually overwhelm my thoughts, and I cause myself more trouble because I cannot seem to make myself relax in the face of difficult, unusual, and unfamiliar shots. In essence, the pros react to vulnerable situations by relaxing a bit, by relying upon feel, while the rest of us poor slobs decide to banish a vulnerable feeling by trying to overpower it. We then compound the problem by convincing ourselves that though this method has not worked in ninety-nine tries, it will surely bring us success the next time.

As always seems to be the case, I realize that I brought this attitude with me the first time I set foot on a golf course. Earlier in my life, when someone hurt my feelings and I started to feel puny, I usually responded by becoming aggressive. I'd do anything to regain some semblance of control. And if I tried my best and still came up short of what I hoped for, I tended to look for someone or something to blame. When that failed, I'd tell myself that it didn't really matter, even though I knew that I was lying to myself. I knew that it's often better to acknowledge feelings of powerlessness and vulnerability than to keep butting my head against the wall, but it was difficult to stop doing it. I also knew that acknowledging my hurt feelings was preferable to looking for a way to get even, but thinking about revenge at least took my mind off the scary feelings for a while.

In cases like this, we'd benefit much more from understanding our feelings and working with what they give us. But doing so would not immediately rid us of feelings that force us to admit that we are not the masters of the universe. We'd much prefer the illusion that we are in charge to the understanding that we haven't a clue what to do. It's a lot like being in a bunker. Getting the vulnerable feeling behind us is uppermost in our minds, whether we're hitting the ball over water or trying to figure out how to avoid telling a friend that we haven't kept a promise.

Because I envy the way that the pros allow themselves to feel vulnerable over certain shots and to perform well because they realize that vulnerability, I wonder if they are better able than most to respond in the same way when vulnerability or powerlessness make appearances in their lives. Maybe they are, though I'm inclined to think that they are just as susceptible to the temptation to fall back on illusions of power when they are threatened in some way, just like the rest of the human race.

Then I think about watching Arnold Palmer at the U.S. Open in 1995. He had received his last special exemption to play in the event, and he struggled valiantly, as he always does. But he and everyone else knew that he had a poor chance even to make the cut, much less to contend for the title. He could have declined the invitation and saved himself the potential embarrassment that a less than stellar performance would bring him. But there he was, sweating away and working like a dog, failing to qualify for the last two rounds. As he walked up the eighteenth fairway on Friday, however, it occurred to me that he was willing to appear so vulnerable because people so much wanted to see him working at it one last time. My guess is that he didn't feel humiliated at all; his game had deteriorated over time, but he appeared more dignified than he had ever been, and that's saying something. As he embraced that vulnerability, he allowed himself to experience the fans' love even more than he had previously, and that is saying something, too.

Nobody likes being vulnerable or powerless, but these feelings are part of the human condition. So when life brings us face to face with them, we have the opportunity to become who we are if we embrace rather than run away from them. In the long run, we are powerless to determine our fate. It sounds scary, but it's really a gift, because it reminds us who we are and who we are not. I still don't much like being in sand traps. But I now try to relax a bit when I'm in that vulnerable position. Each time I do, I am amazed at how much simpler the shot becomes. Vulnerability is an invitation to relax, not a challenge to test our mettle. Yet another mystery that golf makes clearer for us.

8

LETTING GO

Almost every week during the Spring and Summer, little one-day events bring amateurs into the orbit of tour players for a day. Duffers with the right connections (or the right sized checkbook) get to play eighteen holes with a pro, and the public is invited to watch. These little tournaments are very popular, because any hacker knows that few things are more satisfying than watching a good player hit a golf ball. It just so happens that these events also allow the average player to watch some poor amateur play worse than he does. It's a delightful combination.

The other plus is that the tour players are somewhat more accessible on these days. They will stop to sign autographs after holing out, and the more loquacious will even engage in something approaching a conversation. The result is that an addict like me can rub elbows with the great ones and hope that some of the magic will stick.

At least this is what I think about such celebrity golf outings now. In the past, I had presumed that such tournaments served only to pad the pros' pockets with a little unofficial cash. While this is true, I had been unaware of the benefits that could be reaped by a player like me until I attended the Vince Gill tournament outside of Nashville one summer. It was an incredibly hot day and I wilted pretty fast, but my spirits didn't come down for a month or two, because I picked up an insight that I hope will be with me forever.

Watching the pros more than compensated for the heat and the poor play of some of the amateur competitors. As I think about what I saw them do, I now realize that I *knew* this simple truth about golf, but that it didn't really mean much to me until I experienced it firsthand. In other words, I had the image in my mind, but seeing the pros close up breathed life into an idea which had been a pretty sterile concept for me until then.

What I learned began with the sudden understanding that many, if not most, of the pros are my size or smaller (six feet, 180). I suppose that I shouldn't have been surprised when I found myself towering over Robert Gamez. My being taller than he is didn't knock me back too far, but standing next to some other players actually shocked me.

First, there is Lee Janzen. He's about my height, but he's so thin that you'd expect him to qualify for some sort of summer program for disadvantaged youth. His voice is thin, too, and his smile, though friendly, is a bit tentative, as if he expects someone to discover that he has gained admission to the grounds illegally. In other words, you don't find yourself intimidated when you are standing beside him (though other players often feel more than a little threatened when he is closing in on them during a tournament). Russ Cochran is another thin guy, a one iron with legs.

Far more shocking is John Daly, who is actually shorter than I am, though he is more than a tad heavier. When I walked up to the putting green before the round began, he was surrounded by people seeking his autograph, and he seemed to be enjoying it all. He bantered with the crowd and was patient even with people who tended to be pushy. But I just kept staring at him, wondering at how *small* he seemed to be. I probably assumed he'd be as huge as his shots. No one should be able to hit the ball that far without being much bigger than average.

I'd long been aware that size doesn't mean much in golf, but I never paid much attention to that truth. Nobody is more than a few inches high on television, so it's easy to forget that Tom Kite is considerably shorter and lighter than, say, Ernie Els. And though Els is longer off the tee, Kite hits it pretty far, as do Pavin, Henninger, and the other smaller players. As I watched the pros on the practice tee, I saw that, except for Big John, all of them hit the ball about the same. Some were a bit longer than others (perhaps even as much as a full club), but they all hit it pretty far, if you ask me. Put Gamez up against Andy Bean, and it's a toss-up as to who's longer. Pit them against one another, and the size of the heart, rather than the inseam, will make the difference.

Even more striking was the impression that I was watching the action in slow motion. Whether it was Daly hitting a driver or Bob Estes hitting a wedge, all of the swings appeared to take much longer than I had supposed they would. Everything else that happened was as it should be, but the swings that the pros made all seemed to be on tape, and in slow motion.

At first, I attributed this to the sort of double take that one does with the shock of recognition. For a while, I couldn't get over how cool it was to see up close some of the moves that I have become accustomed to seeing only on TV (I am clearly a hopeless, starstruck fan). A good example was Janzen's fidgety preshot routine, complete with laser sighting and total left arm shrug. The first time I saw him do this in person (from a good fifty yards away), I expected an on-course commentator to make a remark. When I heard no play-by-play, I actually supplied some myself (Janzen has 140 yards to the pin. It should just be a comfortable nine iron for him). Janzen did everything I had come to expect, even though I had never been near him before.

So I was thrown for a while, seeing all of these familiar moves in person. I assumed that I had, at least for a while, turned myself into a camera and had decided to preserve the action, take it home with me, and study it later. Only after I had seen most of the field go by did I realize that I was not

in some sort of time warp. With one notable exception
(Lanny Wadkins was there), all of the swings the pros made
were much, much slower than I thought they would be.

Only later did I realize that what I saw as slow motion
was actually rhythm and tempo, two elements of the swing
which I have always found difficult to manage. Of course,
each of the players swung at a somewhat different rate, but
all of them maintained what appeared to be a consistent
speed from the takeaway to the follow-through. In other
words, the clubhead gained plenty of momentum as it
approached the ball, but this had little to do with the speed
of the arms, or the rest of the body for that matter. The
rhythm and tempo that each of them displayed served to
increase the power they generated, but only because they
also managed to do something else.

Each time that I have taken a lesson, I have been told that
I won't experience real success at golf until I learn to relax a
little. I usually don't begin my backswing until I have generated a degree of tension found only in the Middle East,
Bosnia, or some other hotbed of civil strife. The tension
begins with my grip and it eventually finds its way to every
other part of my body, but it does me the greatest damage
just above my hands, in the wrists.

It's not simply that the wrists should *act* as hinges; they
actually *are* hinges. But this little anatomical fact escapes me
every time I pick up a golf club. My wrists, those perfectly
natural hinges, become fused to my hands and forearms,
locked in one position. And I wonder why I don't generate
decent clubhead speed.

A teacher once demonstrated the necessity of letting the
wrists act naturally by swinging two sticks connected by a
couple of links of chain. When he held one of the sticks at
its end and made a swing, the second stick cocked itself on
the backswing and released with a startling amount of speed
as the first stick approached the imaginary ball on the
ground. The first stick represented the arms, and the second

was the club, but the two worked together at optimum efficiency because of the links of chain, which, of course, provided the image of the wrists, doing what they were made to do.

But the wrists can only do what comes naturally to them if I allow them to do so. Because I bring a lot of tension to my swing, I shut the wrists down, freezing them in a remarkably inefficient position. The resulting energy would be hard pressed to run a small flashlight, much less to send a ball at rest speeding far down the fairway, preferably with a slight draw.

As a result of my wrist-locking tendency, my teachers have had to explain, over and over, that I need to pay more attention to letting the wrists go, allowing them to give me power by letting other parts of my body supply it.

They labored in vain for some time, these patient teachers of mine. My wrists were clearly a problem, but my trouble began somewhere else, and only I could get to the source. My wrists could never act as hinges until I changed my basic approach to golf—and to life. From the time I could think, I had always believed that I was supposed to make things happen. I believed that I had the power to manipulate my environment, to take charge and to force the world to conform to my wishes. Despite constant failures to bend the world, or other people, or even myself to my desires, I continued to press ahead. If I didn't accomplish what I had set out to do, I had simply failed to try hard enough.

This goes a long way toward explaining the tension I felt in my hands (and thus the rest of my body) when I stood over a golf ball. If it were to get where I wanted it to go, I would have to force it there, and this meant that I had to work like a demon to get the job done. Of *course* I was tense; everything was up to me.

I have always known that my wrists are not powerful

enough to do what I ask of them. Nobody's wrists are all
that strong, at least compared to other parts of their bodies.
And my wrists are punier than most. So I could have
realized that they can only serve as conduits for the strength
that I generate elsewhere. But it didn't seem to matter.
Though I knew better, I routinely decided to be swayed by
my desires, as if wishing would make them so.

Good players realize that the strength of the swing and
the clubhead speed that they generate come from the
ground up. The legs provide the greatest impetus because
they contain some enormous muscles. And when the rest of
the body allows a smooth transfer of that power from the
legs to the shoulders to the arms to the club, the resulting
speed can send a golf ball a long way. The key is that the
good players put into practice what they know. People like
me spend their golfing lives trying to turn the world of
physics upside down.

Poorer players try to force the issue, try to hit the ball
with their wrists, hands and arms instead of allowing the
wrists and hands to respond to what the rest of the body is
doing. This is why so many hackers look like contortionists
when they swing a golf club. As soon as they bring their
hands and wrists into the swing, they interrupt and eventually spoil what the rest of the body has been trying to do.
The basic result is a slowing down of all of the speed that
the backswing generates, and this redoubles the tendency of
the hands and wrists to compensate for what is being lost.
By the time that the club nears the ball, most of that natural power has been lost. So the wrists and hands, the two
weakest links in the chain of strength, try to regenerate the
power and speed that have already been squandered.

Poor players go a step further by refusing to let the wrists
hinge on their way *back*, or at least by restricting the amount
of hinging. And even if, by some accident, they manage to
get their wrists cocked, they squander all of the benefit this
gives by trying to *make* them release on the way down. Even

the greatest athlete is unable to make his wrists release nearly as quickly as they will on their own, as they respond to the
force being generated by a smooth, rhythmic swing which
begins from the ground up.

Golf teachers constantly face the challenge of helping
their students to *know* and to *accept* this truth. Often, they
ask their students to take half a backswing, allowing the
wrists to cock, and then to swing through the ball, concen-
trating on letting the wrists be the hinges that they naturally are.

Many people have difficulty actually doing this, even
when they try, because the belief that everything is up to
them is so deeply embedded in their psyches. They believe
that they must manipulate the club with the hands and
wrists, just as they must make things happen in any area of
life. But when people manage, through practice, to do what
their teachers have told them, they are usually shocked at
how far (and how fast) the ball travels. But even this experience is not enough for most human beings. They are not
about to allow some actual evidence to affect long-held and
cherished beliefs.

What really shocks people is the sensation that they have
really exerted no effort at all, or at least that they have not
made anything happen. While hitting the ball well feels
good, it results in great confusion, because people don't
believe that life is supposed to be so easy or so free of com-
plication.

Most people struggle to make things happen, and though
they usually fail to work their will, they cling to the belief that
any success must be accompanied by back-breaking efforts.
And, in a strangely masochistic way, failure becomes somewhat satisfying as long as they exhaust themselves in the
process. This, by the way, is a spiritually unhealthy attitude.

During one scene in the movie *Caddyshack*, the character
played by Chevy Chase is giving a lesson in golf and in life
to a younger player. All the while, he bounds around the

putting green, swinging carelessly at balls scattered around and intoning a quasi mantra. All of the putts go in, of course, and the lesson ends as he tells the younger man, "Be the ball, Danny." It's a very funny scene for a number of reasons, not the least of which is that it expresses a truth about golf that everyone knows but that few are able to incorporate into their games. Golf, above all else, demands a curious mixture of concentration and letting go, of focus and relaxation, of desire and lack of desire. Because good golf depends upon this blend, it offers the player an important insight into the nature of mystery.

If you read any golf instruction, you have to be astounded by the many parts which must work together if a player is to achieve any success at all. It is a complicated game, one that demands hours of practice, even if one is a good athlete to begin with. Of course, the result of all of the various tips that good players and teachers give is that lesser players are easily confused and overwhelmed. There is so much to know, so much to learn, so much to practice. Poorer players tend to be on the lookout for the key, a swing mechanic or a brand of irons that will make it all come together. Unfortunately, such a key does not exist, as any good player could tell them. At least it doesn't exist in a manual or on a pro shop shelf.

If there is a key to the game, it lives deep within anyone who picks up a club. The key consists in both knowing and trusting that good golf comes to those who can both concentrate *and* let go, who can both focus on what they are doing *and* allow themselves to do what comes naturally. Golf, in other words, demands that we stop trying to *make* things so that we can *let* things happen.

This truth is implied by players who work to clear their heads of swing thoughts before they take the club back. The best players will try to focus upon one swing thought, or two at the most. And these thoughts have nothing to do with power or speed. Instead, helpful swing thoughts might involve getting started slowly or straight back, or making a good shoulder turn, or making sure that the backswing is complete. As they begin their swings, they try to banish other thoughts from their minds, because they know that the more they work at *making* things happen, the less they will be able to *let* them happen.

I think this is why everyone has a preshot routine these days. As poorer players have been exposed to wider golf coverage, they have seen that good players go through a series of actions as they prepare to play a shot. So everyone has developed a preshot routine by emulating good players. Unfortunately, most people have difficulty incorporating the mindset that should accompany such a warm-up procedure.

They don't realize, for example, that good players use this time to focus upon the task at hand and that they accomplish this by going through repeatable steps that clear their minds of extraneous thoughts (like the double bogey they just made or the difficult hole they will have to play later in the round). Finally, all the good players seem to have a trigger, a motion with which they begin the swing. From then on, they let the years of practice take over; though they may have that one swing thought in mind, they use it simply to put into motion a swing which they have honed through countless hours of practice.

When you think about it, this decision to keep things simple and to allow the swing to happen flows from the player's need to allow so many parts of his or her body to act in harmony with one another. Since it is impossible for anyone to concentrate that much, golfers must not focus upon trying to *achieve* harmony, because harmony can only occur if we trust all the years of practice, during which we patiently learned the many components that result in a good pass at the ball. So we put everything into motion after clearing our minds and bodies of as many obstacles as possible; once the swing process begins, we let go and allow the swing to happen.

At least that's the way I see it. God knows, all of my trying to force a good swing from a confused jumble of body movements and a million different (and often contradictory) thoughts hasn't gotten me anywhere. And it always happens that the more I want to get it right, the less likely I am to get it right. In other words, the *desire* to hit the ball correctly gets in the way of my actually hitting it correctly. Desire isn't necessarily a bad thing, of course, but unshackled desire always cripples us by increasing the tension as the stakes become higher. The more we want something, the more we come to believe that it depends upon us and our efforts. The harder we try, the more difficult it becomes to let our natural gifts come into play. We become convinced that we cannot achieve anything that we desire, when the truth is that we have all the necessary gifts to accomplish the task. We simply need to relax and let them work for us.

When children learn to walk, they experience all sorts of little mishaps along the way. The first time that they stand alone, unaided by any outside balancing tool (say, a couch), you can see them become somewhat disoriented. Then their legs, which have those enormous muscles we all know about, buckle. Interestingly enough, they usually find themselves standing erect without trying to accomplish this marvelous trick, and they only waver when they realize what they are doing and presume that they shouldn't be able to.

Soon enough, when they decide to trust their natural gift for balance, they are off to the races. We look in wonder as children learn to crawl, balance themselves, walk and then run, moving from one step to the next as they trust the newest bit of learning.

Eventually, we all learn to walk and run, and from then on, we perform these marvels without thinking about them much at all, without remembering that our ability to perform them increased the less we worried about them. All of the parts work together, each adding its own piece to a very complicated puzzle, but the complete task becomes simple precisely because we aren't trying to think about doing it.

The result is that we learn to walk by trusting the smoothly coordinated components that are involved. Then we spend the rest of our lives forgetting that we know how to let things happen. Whether we are trying to learn how to swing a golf club or going about the business of being parents, brothers, sisters, or friends, we allow desire to uncoordinate us, and the result is a confused jumble of missteps. As often as not, our false steps result from the belief that everything is up to us, and this attitude breeds fear, especially the fear that we are not up to the task. This is why we either walk away, giving up because we don't believe we have what is required, or try harder, increasing the tension and digging ever bigger holes for ourselves.

Something strange happened one evening when I went out to my car. As I got in, I was running through my mental grocery checklist, but just before I turned the key in the ignition, I suddenly realized that I had no memory of putting the key in. Though it was dark, and though I had to reach around the steering wheel, I had managed to put the key into the ignition the first time without thinking about it at all. Because I was surprised about it, I took the key out and tried it again, and I needed three attempts to accomplish what I had done without thinking the first time.

I have done this hundreds of times, of course. In fact, I perform many daily tasks without thinking about them at all, even though they are relatively complicated procedures. But if I pay too close attention to what I am doing, I actually slow myself down. Or I discover that they are somewhat more difficult to accomplish because I am *trying* to do them. When I fall back on automatic pilot, perfected through hundreds or thousands of repetitions, I work smoothly, without a hitch. I am a virtuoso, and I don't even know it.

In the same way, our relationships sometimes suffer because we fail to fall back on our experience. We often overanalyze the events of our lives, making much more of them than they really are or trying to reinvent the wheel each time something out of the ordinary happens. While this does not mean that life should be a series of instantaneous, knee-jerk reactions, it does indicate, I think, that a certain amount of letting go, of allowing ourselves to be ourselves, is necessary if we wish to experience fulfillment. No amount of analysis can eliminate the need to fall back upon what comes naturally. In the long run, the purpose of analysis should often be to rid ourselves of what *doesn't* come naturally.

For example, people often confuse their natural inclination to compassion with a belief that they are responsible for others, and this causes them to create pain (for themselves and others) where there was none before. More often than not, the desire to control events springs from the desire that the people we love be happy and fulfilled. But if we come to believe that we are responsible for that happiness or fulfillment, we will (knowingly or unknowingly) impinge on their freedom. Our intentions may be pure, but they are sullied by desire and by our belief that someone's happiness depends upon us. Relationships become confusing and painful, all because we do the equivalent of locking our wrists during the backswing.

Many of the mistakes we make in relationships arise out of our worries about "performing" well, but if we learn anything at all from those mistakes, we may discover that our relationships thrive when we forget about performing and decide to be ourselves. We need only realize that our greatest mistake is failing to trust the gifts we have been given, failing to see that we have what we need to find and nurture the relationships that can sustain us. But like small children, we find ourselves making the same mistakes over and over, and we risk losing totally our faith in the gifts we've had from the start but have forgotten how to use. And we forget how to use them because we are *trying* so hard.

If you watch enough golf, you see evidence that players sometimes get into what they call a zone. On days like that, all the drives are in the fairway, the short game is sharp, and every putt seems to drop. If a player who's having such a day gets into deep trouble, she or he will usually find a way out or at the very least won't allow one shot to destroy the entire round.

All the pros began their golfing lives with some natural talent, and they put themselves in the hands of wise teachers who helped them to get the most out of it. Then they practiced for years. For each of them, one or another facet of the game comes more easily. And then, every once in a while, it all comes together. They know that their talent, their lessons, and their hard work are paying off, but they really can't quite figure out how they have reached the zone that they find themselves in. If they are asked, they can only describe it in images and vague or tentative words.

The way I see it, everything comes together for them because they are somehow doing a better job of letting go, of trusting their talents and trying not to force them to work. Even great players have relatively few times like this because they are human beings, and human beings find it difficult to let go, to *allow* things to happen rather than believing that they must *make* them happen. They go through their routines as they have thousands of times before, and they may even have a swing thought or two; but once they start back, they allow themselves to trust their talent and their lessons better than usual, and it all falls into place.

Other areas of life are much the same. When people in trouble of some kind come to talk with me, I have to watch myself. Because I care, I can find myself allowing my desire to help them get in the way of actually being of any assistance to them. The more I want their troubles to disappear, the more likely I am to try to *make* them disappear. And I can accomplish this artificial task in many ways, especially by telling them what to do. Nobody ever gained much by letting somebody else live her life for her, however, so I find that I do much more for people by displaying some compassion than by giving them a checklist of healthy or unhealthy behaviors. If I help them to focus upon the real issues, they will ordinarily find that they have what they need to address them.

On the other hand, people in trouble often are *looking* for someone to tell them what to do. When this is their desire, it is often a result of their trying so hard to resolve a problem that they have become hopelessly confused. A truly compassionate friend will accompany a person in need through the quicksand of terrifying feelings (or find someone who can) rather than assisting the person to run away from those feelings.

Being of help to people and getting assistance from people require the same kind of letting go. We are our best selves when we realize that we have what we need to love the people in our lives and to allow them to love us. It's only when we try to force things that our relationships go sour and become confused.

The talents that people bring to relationships differ, and no one lets go all of the time. Life is a process of learning that we thrive when we find a balance between desire and lack of desire, a balance between developing our gifts and then trusting them. In the same way, the best players are the ones who learn to do this balancing act on the course, but none of them get it right all of the time. In fact, getting it *right* isn't the point at all. Letting it *happen* is the idea, but we have to avoid falling into the trap of believing we can *make* ourselves do it. We're on our way when we accept that. It's also important to remember that we're never far from the temptation to take it back all over again.

All players bring with them some desire for control when they tee it up. The good players are the ones who can bracket that desire to some degree, at least when they're out on the course. And because they have seized the opportunity that golf presents them in this regard, they have at least a decent chance of taking what they've learned to their relationships.

There is no guarantee, however. Because people tend to compartmentalize their lives, even very good players can easily miss the lessons that golf places right in front of them. When they're playing golf, they may very well think that this is all they are doing. If they opened their eyes a bit, they might see that the game also offers their spirits a little room to grow. Golf can help us recognize that we cannot force or control the mystery that surrounds us and lives within us. We can only cooperate with it, but this involves a letting go of desire. Hitting a golf ball well might allow us to trust the mystery a little better, as long as we accept the invitation to let go.

9

SCORECARD

A few years ago, I saw a number of advertisements about a national "play Fred Couples" day. The idea was that anyone with an established handicap could play a round at his or her own course on a set day. The adjusted scores would then be compared to Freddie's round on that day. Though I can't remember who sponsored the event or what prizes were to be awarded, the event amused me.

Any serious player has played a match against Couples or Nicklaus or any of the big stars hundreds of times. It's like the golf advertisement where the kid, out on the course by himself, is playing for the PGA championship. He stands over the ball on eighteen, saying to himself, "He's hit his drive fifty yards past Freddie." As the shot leaves his club and sails for the green, his voice is the epitome of hard-won and very satisfied achievement: "It looks like we've got ourselves a new PGA champion."

Anyone who's really into the game has secret battles against the great players. And despite the appearances, these make-believe contests are not necessarily pitiable attempts to rise above painfully dull lives, though they might help. Instead, they can act as incentives to concentrate better, to improve course management, or to forget about dreadfully hot weather. I've won countless U.S. Opens; all of the great ones have looked on in envy and awe as I have come from behind (I *always* come from behind) to take the title.

Creating a fairy tale is a wonderful and inexpensive way to salvage an otherwise forgettable round of golf.

Such make-believe games are a tradition in sports. When my friends and I played pick-up baseball games in grade school, it was always the seventh game of the World Series. And our marathon Sunday football games were more than a bunch of sixteen- and seventeen-year-olds getting together to bash in each other's skulls. Whether we said it out loud or not, we were playing for the NFL championship (until pro football ushered us into the age of Super Bowls). The games we played transported us beyond the school yards where we gathered to the great arenas and ball yards of the big time. And everyone was a star.

But the contest against Fred Couples was different. Everyone in the country had the opportunity actually to play against him, and because of the handicap system, even the poorest players had a reasonable chance to beat him. It was an intriguing prospect. Because golf is the game it is, anyone with a set of clubs has the opportunity to put his or her game up against one of the best players in the world without inviting ridicule. This wasn't fantasy; it was a real contest.

Only golf could sustain such an event. It's one thing for a fifteen-year-old kid to pretend that he's facing Randy Johnson; it's something else (suicide, most likely) if it's the real thing. At best, it's fair to say that the average person would have no chance to do much with a Johnson fast ball (except to watch it sail by or avoid being knocked senseless). How about a "run through the 49ers' defensive line" contest? Or a "stand in the way of a Pete Sampras serve" game of tennis? You'd like, perhaps, to be goalie for a day and let Eric Lindros or Sergei Fedorov come at you?

In other sports, fantasy is the only option. If you don't have the talent to get out on the ice, or the court, or the field, then you shouldn't step over the railing. You could be injured or killed. At the very least, you'd be embarrassed to death. It's much safer, not to mention more rewarding, to win the French Open from the quiet of your den or the local asphalt court, than to stand out there in front of all of those people and fail miserably.

So one summer day a few years ago, all sorts of people played eighteen holes against Fred Couples. I never heard the results, but I suspect that a fair number of the contestants beat him. And they accomplished this without any subterfuge or the use of mirrors. The results were certified by a system that is unique in sports (if, like me, you don't count bowling).

I don't know why or how the handicap system came into existence, but I imagine that it had something to do with the understanding that golf is an easy game to play poorly, but an impossible one to master. People of all skill levels must play the same layouts. Par remains the same for everyone, so moving up the tee markers is not enough to level the playing field, as sports announcers never tire of saying.

Perhaps the most important reason for the development of the handicap system, however, is the understanding that everyone plays against the course first. Regardless of who wins or loses, everyone's score is measured against par. So the handicap system adjusts par for people of different abilities, and the result is that anyone who's having a reasonably good day can beat Fred Couples. In any event, everyone knows that the course, even though it may lose a few battles, always wins the war.

Several years ago, when I lived in another town, three friends and I would get together at least once a month to play. Because two of the guys are accountants, the betting was rather elaborate, and those two had to be on different teams to avoid the appearance of collusion. Points were awarded or lost for sneaks (getting a par when you weren't on the green in regulation) and snakes (three putts), closest to the hole in regulation, the rare birdie, polies (a putt longer than the flag stick), and any number of other accomplishments. But all of this was contested against the background of the handicap that each of us brought to the course.

It continues to amaze me that the handicap was a given. We might complain a bit if one player had a particularly good day and played much better than his handicap indicated, but we knew that it happens. Each of us managed to do it at one time or another. The handicap was simply an undisputed fact of the game, like the common understanding that shorter people should be allowed to stand at the front of a crowd and that doorways should be built to accommodate people who are taller than average (NBA players excepted).

What's sad about this is that most players fail to take what they accept without question on the golf course and apply it to the rest of life. It's so easy for us to think that we deserve our handicap on the golf course, but that no one else deserves a break anywhere else.

Maybe that's why people like to use other sports as metaphors for life. All of that talk about teamwork and sacrificing oneself for the good of others is a great way to justify life as it is. This is not to say that sacrifice and teamwork are bad things. It's just that we prefer to see someone else doing the sacrificing most of the time.

On the other hand, the handicap system provides us with a look at the way life could be. If this is so, then maybe we avoid applying it as an image for other areas of life because it might necessitate our entertaining the notion that a few changes in standard procedure could be good for everyone. Perhaps we don't think about what the handicap system has to offer, treating it as an idiosyncrasy of golf which has no application to the wider world.

We might get a better idea of what an important gift the handicap system is if we imagined the game without it. In the absence of the system, the differences in skill levels would be underscored by the focus on the player's raw, unadjusted score. Everything would change, especially the understanding that people play the course as well as each other. This would introduce the unhealthy competitive edge that has turned so many other games into a constant display of one-upmanship and a series of "see how much better I am" sideshows.

I don't know whether such grandstanding originated in sports and then filtered into the rest of our lives or vice versa. Either way, it's not good for our souls. In so many ways, golf teaches very different lessons. They are lessons that would bring us closer to each other and closer to ourselves as we were made to be, if we took them home with us.

The handicap system is just one of these lessons, but it is a vital one. We have, in the recent past, made provisions for people who have difficulty getting around in a world that the rest of us negotiate with ease. Wheelchair ramps and Braille script on elevators are simple enough to provide for people, but they are expensive, and a good number of us resent all of this effort in time and money on behalf of a relative few people. If we had heeded the lessons of golf's handicap system, we'd have built in these aids a long time ago. Now that we are beginning to catch up, we ought to be thankful that we've finally come around to a more compassionate way of looking at each other, instead of carping about "special favors" that some people are getting. When we are in this mode, by the way, it's always someone else who is getting the "special favors." This should tell us something.

Golf has been granting such special favors for quite a while now, and it has done so because it recognizes that very few people have complete games. One of the members of the foursome I spoke of a while back has a really unorthodox swing. As a result, he does not hit the ball very far at all. But he can putt like a demon, and his handicap has allowed that great putting stroke to take some money out of my pocket.

At times, after he has rolled in a long one, I have found myself momentarily cursing the handicap system, but I must admit that it forces me to acknowledge his skill on the greens. Without his handicap, I'd be content to see him make every putt in sight, because his great putting wouldn't cost me anything at all. Because the handicap allows him to play even up, his skill means something when we are playing. And I am forced (if that's what it takes) to admire, acknowledge, and appreciate his talent with the putter.

Out there in the real world, the attention and adulation tend to go to the big hitters, the people who can bring power to bear in all situations. This is a spiritually unhealthy situation, an altar at which golf refuses to worship. Even when people of essentially equal skills get together, power players don't necessarily have an advantage, because the short game can make up for a lack of distance off the tee, and accurate irons can, too. Golf isn't all about power and pizzazz, and life isn't meant to be either. So golf honors whatever skills a player brings to it by implementing a system which gives those skills a chance to make a difference, even if the opponent is Fred Couples.

Life as we live it these days is very much the opposite. It tends to reward those who have the power to make themselves visible, and it seeks out weaknesses in everybody else. Maybe we'd be better off if we tried to recognize individual gifts in people instead of insisting that they either develop the ones we consider important or find a seat at the back of the bus, so to speak. Maybe the gifts which we fail to see or to appreciate could make a difference in the world. The tradition of golf would say that people ought to be given an even chance to display their gifts; it begins by acknowledging that those gifts are important and do make a difference, that they deserve just as much respect as the flashier skills of a relative few.

It's really a fair system. As one's abilities increase, his handicap goes down. But if he runs into a rough patch, the system gives him a break for a time. The result is that everyone can compete, and although anyone might win, the good players still have a better than even chance of coming out on top. After all, not everyone who took on Freddie a couple of summers ago cleaned his clock. I suspect that he survived being bested by a few hackers anyway. He knows well enough that they had to bring more than luck and their handicaps to the competition. Each, in his own way, brought some talent along with him. Golf simply allowed these people to use those skills in an even match. The handicap system is part of a larger tradition in golf which makes it the most spiritual of games. You can see examples of this all over the place, if you're willing to take a closer look.

Anyone who thinks that golf is a game like other games would almost certainly have to reevaluate his position after watching the 1995 U.S. Open. In many ways, it was like any Open of the past: the course was difficult but fair, par was hard to achieve, they kept score, and a winner was declared. But because many other things happened, right there on national TV, the viewer was left with the distinct impression that the rewards of playing the game include more than just winning.

Perhaps the problem is that we tend to live by the old maxim, attributed to Vince Lombardi, that "winning isn't everything; it's the only thing." Whether we are watching football, basketball, or golf, the emphasis always seems to be who wins. Everybody else loses and is somehow less than those who triumph. Almost isn't good enough.

Contrast that with an event that occurred early in the tournament. As Greg Norman was preparing to hit a tee shot on Thursday, Ray Floyd, who was in his group, suddenly spoke up and told him to wait. Someone, a fan or a journalist, was snapping a picture, or at least preparing to do so. Floyd didn't want this to happen during Norman's swing. This was, on the face of it, a remarkable episode, because athletes in other sports would have considered it insanity. They would have been more than content to let folks take all the pictures they wanted, at least when their opponents were preparing to hit the ball. There would be hell to pay, however, if anyone dared to interrupt them.

One of the on-course commentators later said that as Norman walked down the fairway, he told Paul Azinger, the other member of the group, that he'd never seen anything like this in another sport. And he's right, of course. In other sports, the fans even get into the act, slapping the glass as opposing players skate by or waving their arms (or whatever else they can get aloft) as the opposing team is attempting free throws.

Throughout the round and the entire tournament, Floyd could be heard as he urged his playing companions' putts to drop or chips to get close. While a cynic could say that Floyd had no chance to win the tournament and could thus afford to become a sort of cheerleader, that wasn't the case at all, as any golfer knows.

At any level of competition, from the Open to a junior tournament in Iowa to weekend competitions between friends, it is routine for players to compliment a shot by an opponent, even if he is threatening to bury the rest of the field. No matter what's at stake, golfers prize good play, no matter whose play it is. And they're not shy about saying so. Neither are the compliments hollow, a screen for dark thoughts about a desired collapse by the opponent. Golf simply doesn't allow for this line of thinking.

Every once in a while, I see advertisements that end with the line, "Join the people who think that golf is more than just a game." No other sport could promote itself with such a line, because no other game has so many built-in rewards that have little or nothing to do with winning. Virtually everything about golf points to the intangible but very real benefits which a person can take back into the rest of his life. Appreciation for the achievements of others is one of them, and this book has been filled, I hope, with others. Golf doesn't have room for many of the self-promoting, anything-for-a-victory attitudes which prevail in other games.

But the rest of the world certainly does. That year's Open once again provided the raw materials for those who have made a sort of cottage industry out of talking about Norman's "failures" in major tournaments. There he was, second again. Always a bridesmaid, never a bride, and so on. All of these stories were based upon the understanding that first place is the only place to be and that anything else is "failure." After the tournament was over (by the way, I love the way Norman pronounces the word "tournament"), all of the old "failures" were dragged out, dusted off, and commented upon. If winning were the only benefit to be gained from teeing it up, all of these stories would be valid.

Yet he insisted that he was fine, that he had done his best, and he offered warm and evidently sincere congratulations to Corey Pavin. Surely, this was an example of world-class denial or of trying to salvage something, anything, worthwhile out of an otherwise devastating experience. A lot of people might well have thought that when he said, "Welcome to the club," a reference to his British Open titles, he was anticipating his critics and reminding them that he was not the loser that they seem to think he is.

But I don't think so. In a televised interview earlier in the week, he had said something that gets to the heart of golf, something that has apparently sustained him through all of the criticism and the disappointments. In essence, he told the interviewer that golf allows a person to learn things that carry over into life, that he is a better person these days, not just because he has two major titles and another sixty or so worldwide, but because he has, despite his best efforts, come up short a lot of times, too.

In saying this, he demonstrated that he understands very well the spiritual benefits of the game. And spiritual benefits are not meant to soothe the ego of a person who knows that he is a loser. Okay, I know that they keep score in golf, too, and that only one name goes on the trophy. I also know that anyone who has ever picked up a club, myself included, dreams of winning the Open some day. But golf, at any level, offers a player more than that.

Greg Norman was saying that he has learned some pretty important lessons, about golf and about life, and he has learned them the only way possible, through sometimes painful experience. As a result, he knows as well as anyone that all he can do is the best he can do. Success cannot be measured solely by whose name goes on the trophy, and there is satisfaction in performing to the best of one's abilities, no matter the outcome. The world calls this a hollow victory or wishful thinking or plain foolishness, but people who play golf should understand that this is not the case at all.

People who want to define Norman as some sort of tragic figure, one who comes close but never reaches the prize (which, considering his many victories, is pretty foolish all by itself), fail to appreciate golf for what it is. It's not simply a game to determine who wins and who loses. It's an endeavor that seeks to bring out the best in people. The competition is grueling, but the competitors are not enemies. The prize is clear, but it is not to be taken at all costs. And the game awards more than the low score.

When Paul Azinger holed a bunker shot at eighteen during the last round of the Memorial Tournament a few years ago, he experienced a rush of two distinct feelings, each of them intense. He was, of course, thrilled to win the event, but he also knew that his shot was a knife to the heart of Payne Stewart, his nearest rival at the time and his closest friend on tour. While he didn't even consider returning the trophy, he was consumed with feelings for Stewart. In part, this was a result of having been in his friend's position a time or two; but it was also an indication that golf promotes just this sort of appreciation for what the other players are experiencing.

Norman, Azinger, and all of those who compete at their level have this same appreciation because the game demands it. And anyone who plays golf has opportunities to ponder the truth that there is much more to the game than simply taking home the prize. This does not mean, of course, that Norman doesn't want very much to win an Open, or the Masters, or the PGA. It does not mean that these aren't among his hopes for the future. It also doesn't mean that winning tournaments is not among Paul Azinger's desires whenever he tees it up. It simply means they understand that golf provides them with more than a series of opportunities to get their names on some trophy or other.

While winning remains important to anyone on the tour, it cannot be sought at the expense of the infinitely more important gifts which golf offers. Players who do their best, who play within the rules, who recognize and applaud the achievements of others stand to gain much more than a first prize. They also learn, over and over again, that golf is not so much a contest as a common struggle to engage the game itself. In a very real sense, there are no winners or losers; everyone receives the satisfaction of being part of something much bigger than themselves, and everyone learns that the greatest reward lies in the striving, regardless of the outcome.

More than any other game, golf teaches that winning isn't the greatest prize. Anyone who plays can, if he or she pays attention, learn to appreciate the value of doing one's best and letting it go at that, without regret and without seeing the winners as people to be envied, hated, or feared. Try thinking about football or hockey players calling their opponents "fellow competitors." I suspect that they have far more colorful ways of identifying the people they compete against. Try imagining corporate leaders applauding, rather than cursing, the advances patented by a rival firm.

It might be easier for me and my friends to appreciate all

of this stuff about engaging the game than it is for the pros, since we never compete for anything more than a few dollars at a time. Yet we, too, can become so caught up in the belief that winning is all there is to work for that we leave the course none the wiser for the experience. That's why the handicap system is so important to us. Since it urges us to recognize the course as the common opponent, it also gives us the opportunity to remember that comparing ourselves to each other is a big mistake, one that is bound to put us at odds with each other.

It turns out that the handicap system does more than teach us to appreciate the skills of other people. It also reminds us that when we put the numbers on the scorecard, we are not so much measuring ourselves against each other as viewing our own scores as the measure of who we are and who we hope to be. Our scores remind us of our talents and the areas that need more work. The idea isn't to become better than everybody else. It's to reach our potential, whatever that might be.

Whether my friends and I are bringing our ample handicaps to the friendly little games we play or the best players in the world are competing for the U.S. or British Open, golf reminds us of some important truths. The game encourages us to celebrate the successes and achievements of others, to understand that life is not a contest whose aim is to label people as winners and losers, but a common struggle to use what we have been given, to strive to do our best. We discover ourselves in the midst of that struggle. If we give in to the temptation to believe that the occasional success defines us, we are headed for big trouble, because we experience a lot more failures than triumphs.

Golf teaches that the striving is the only worthwhile enterprise. Absolutely no one can afford to claim that he has no more need to work on his game, regardless of his successes, or that she has nothing more to learn. Success is not measured solely in victories; instead, it is measured by the decision, often unbearably difficult, to keep trying when nothing seems to work, when even one's best efforts do not produce the desired results.

The world at large doesn't care to reward such an attitude. But then the world at large thinks that being the best is the only desirable goal. It fails to mention that only one person can lay claim to that title, and that the rest of us are out of luck. This, perhaps more than anything else, is why golf is such an invaluable spiritual gift.

MAKING THE TURN

I carry about ten ball mark repair tools in my golf bag. I absolutely love to repair ball marks, because having to fix them means that I have hit a good approach. Even when I have chipped from only a few yards off the green, I search carefully for any indication that my shot has dented the turf. Sometimes I have to look for a minute or two to find it, but it's always worth the effort. Repairing ball marks is like having a drink; I always feel better after I do it.

Unfortunately, however, I don't get as many chances as I would like to use all of those tools I carry around. Since my game is erratic, I often tend to bounce or roll the ball onto the green rather than to hit a high iron shot designed to tear up the surface. But I can still repair the marks left by other, less thoughtful (or less compulsive) players. If I am having a good day, I can find at least one such leftover on every green. Though I admit that the satisfaction I get from fixing the ball marks left by others is not as great as fixing those I've made on my own, I still get a vicarious thrill out of the task.

When I can find no ball marks to repair, I go about other little duties. Usually, I can find some sand to sweep off the green. If that fails, there is always the stray leaf or the odd bird dropping (nothing is beneath me in this regard). I have, in short, never met a green that I couldn't somehow improve.

I think that I got into this routine for a couple of reasons. In the first place, I like the world to be neat. Messes indicate a lack of concern for detail. A good bit of my life has been devoted to detecting and then eliminating flaws of one kind or another (sometimes even my own). But I suppose that I have become so fastidious on the golf course because it takes my mind off the shot that I have just hit. When I'm in my cleaning-up mode, everything else fades into the background.

And then there are spike marks. When I took up the game in my early teens, I immediately began flattening out spike marks. I don't remember for sure, but I am willing to bet (given my penchant for neatness) that it was the first thing I did when I reached the green of the very first hole I played. I had not been doing this for long when someone told me that I was not allowed to tamp them down if they were along the line of my putt.

This confused me. After watching golf on TV, I had concluded that while golfers did not know how to dress, they had a mania for neatness, much like my own. They were always removing spike marks, sand, leaves and the like from the greens. I was simply following their lead and satisfying my own compulsion. But after someone warned me not to fool with spike marks, I began to pay closer attention to the players on television. Sure enough, they only repaired spike marks *after* they putted out. But I was still confused.

I suppose that the rule exists to prevent players from "repairing" spike marks all the way from the hole back to the ball, thus building a trench through which the ball could travel on its way into the cup. Perhaps a player with a good eye could fix only certain spike marks and leave a path much like that which a pinball follows on its way to the flippers. That would be fun to see.

But golf isn't supposed to be fun. So you can't repair spike marks. When I watch a tournament on TV, I can sometimes tell that the players really *want* to repair them, at least from time to time. They check ever so carefully to see if a spike mark has become a loose impediment. When the bit of grass comes right up, I can almost see the gleam of triumph in the player's eyes. "Got you, you little bastard."

More often than not, however, the grass isn't loose at all, and the player must either putt right over it or figure a way around it (more or less speed, perhaps). So every weekend, we see a player flattening out a spike mark that has knocked his putt off line, and the emotion with which this is done can be felt hundreds of miles away. I can still picture the disgust on Jack Nicklaus' face after his putt for par on the twelfth at Augusta was sent off line by a spike mark during the final round in 1986. Considering the size of the putter he was using that year, he probably flattened about a dozen of them when he went after the one that affected his otherwise well-struck putt.

Television has brought this right into our dens. We've all seen the camera shot from behind the player, at ground level, the visual that Gary McCord likes to call the "worm cam." Sometimes, the number of spike marks is staggering. It's as if the player has to maneuver through a mine field. No matter what he does, his ball is certain to hit at least one of the marks. It's a wonder that anyone ever makes a putt of more than two feet.

A cursory look at the rules of the game reveals no mention of spike marks. Maybe they didn't have spikes when people were coming up with the rules. In any event, I know that there's some talk about allowing players to repair them; some courses are experimenting with a new type of shoe that doesn't leave marks. All of this has come about because there is a general sentiment that it is inherently unfair to prohibit players from repairing or otherwise fixing spike marks.

I have to say that I'm not all that interested in this debate. The greens on most of the courses I play are so hard that a person's spikes don't even begin to dent the green or to disturb what passes for grass. And when I get to play on a good course, I sort of like to see the spike marks. They remind me that I'm playing on a beautiful and well-maintained course, and they occasionally knock one of my poorer efforts into the hole. Spike marks don't bother me at all.

Well, they *used* to bother me, back in the days when I liked to emulate the great players. Since they made such a big deal about spike marks, I did, too. Then one day, as I was complaining to my playing partners about the spike marks left by the group in front of us, one of them pointed out that I was dragging my feet across the green. I wasn't just making spike marks; I was making spike *tracks*. The green looked as if it had been strafed by tiny F-16's.

Once again, I had been reminded that I specialize in complaining about the faults of others when I actually share the fault in question. And it's true that no matter how hard you try to step lightly, you're bound to leave a spike mark or two. The only way that they could be eliminated would be for every golfer to walk backwards off every green, repairing the marks he has created. I'm not expecting this to happen any time soon.

One solution to the problem is to ignore the rule. If there is an especially offensive spike mark in the way, just tamp it down. What's the big deal? But if we do this, we miss yet another great opportunity to experience a spiritual truth. In this world, we must always deal with whatever has been left behind by those who came before us. Sometimes we call these people benefactors, but sometimes they are thoughtless, greedy, insensitive, or just plain messy. Regardless, they leave a legacy, and we must figure out what to do with it. It's interesting, I think, that we rarely remember to thank those who leave us no mess to clean up, but we *always* curse those who leave the work to us.

If the tournament is on the line, I doubt that any pro who is in the hunt is wasting time thinking about good or bad legacies. But it is true that following the rule and living with the spike marks can teach us to be careful about what we leave behind, on the green and everywhere else, too. It can also remind us that no matter how careful we think we are being, we are likely leaving some sort of mess behind, one that someone else will have to deal with. Keeping this in mind might just help us become a tad less judgmental.

I've now come to the point in this book where I would do well to assess what *I'm* leaving behind. When I told some of my friends that I was planning to write this book, I got a variety of reactions. As I mentioned in the prologue, one of my good friends (and a very spiritual person) told me that trying to make a connection between golf and the spiritual life might be a stretch. Several other people said they were intrigued by the idea, but their faces told me that they thought it was a long shot. Well, here I am, writing the epilogue to a book that demonstrates, I hope, that there is such a connection (so there). I don't want to make more of golf than it is; instead, it has been my intention to make clearer some of the benefits that the game provides to a person willing to take a closer look.

Anyway, most of my friends also suggested that the book be divided into eighteen chapters, and I must admit that I thought so, too. Such a format would have provided me with ready-made chapter titles. I could, for example, have named each chapter after a famous hole on one or another of the most well-known courses around the world. The first chapter might have been called "Number One at Riviera," and subsequent chapters might have included the twelfth at Augusta, the seventeenth at St. Andrews, and the eighteenth at Pebble Beach. Such chapter titles would have served as a good excuse to add some class to the book by including beautiful pictures of lush fairways, undulating greens, and frightening pot bunkers. It was an intriguing concept. Despite some of the obvious advantages of structuring the book in this way, however, I decided to end after nine chapters for two very good reasons.

In the first place, I find myself at an awkward period in my life, a time when I cannot shoot my age or better unless I quit at the turn. Considering the shape of my game, I will be well into my eighties before I can do this, assuming that my skills don't diminish too much. Still, I hope that I will have many, many opportunities to give it a try. This does not mean, of course, that I must wait that long to publish a sequel of nine more chapters. It means simply that I need a bit of a break between nines to allow myself the illusion that I am shooting my age again. This leads directly to the second reason I have decided to stop after nine chapters.

I do intend someday to write a sequel which I hope the world will be eagerly awaiting. Since I don't want to disappoint anyone, I will have to play an awful lot of golf and engage in quite a bit of meditation, but I am willing to make the sacrifice. Both the game of golf and an anxious public deserve nothing less than my best efforts. As the mystery unfolds and makes itself known, I promise to pass everything along. And each time I go out to encounter the mystery, I plan to say that I'm doing research.